ABIDING IN THE SUPERNATURAL

CHINEDU DANIEL OBASI

TEACH Services, Inc.
PUBLISHING
www.TEACHServices.com • (800) 367-1844

World rights reserved. This book or any portion thereof may not be copied or reproduced in any form or manner whatever, except as provided by law, without the written permission of the publisher, except by a reviewer who may quote brief passages in a review.

The author assumes full responsibility for the accuracy and interpretation of the Ellen White quotations cited in this book. Unless otherwise indicated, all scripture quotations are taken from the King James Version of the Bible.

The ESV® Bible (The Holy Bible, English Standard Version®). ESV® Text Edition: 2016. Copyright © 2001 by Crossway, a publishing ministry of Good News Publishers. The ESV® text has been reproduced in cooperation with and by permission of Good News Publishers. Unauthorized reproduction of this publication is prohibited. All rights reserved.

THE HOLY BIBLE, NEW INTERNATIONAL VERSION®, NIV® Copyright © 1973, 1978, 1984, 2011 by Biblica, Inc.™ Used by permission. All rights reserved worldwide.

Passages labeled (AMP) are taken from the Amplified Bible. All rights reserved. For Permission To Quote information visit http://www.lockman.org. The "Amplified" trademark is registered in the United States Patent and Trademark Office by The Lockman Foundation. Use of this trademark requires the permission of The Lockman Foundation.

Passages labeled (TLNT) are taken from the Theological Lexicon of the New Testament, ©1995 by Hendrickson Publications.

Passages labeled (WEB) are taken from the World English Bible. Public domain.

Copyright © 2019 Chinedu Daniel Obasi

Copyright © 2019 TEACH Services, Inc.

ISBN-13: 978-1-4796-0999-4 (Paperback)

ISBN-13: 978-1-4796-1000-6 (ePub)

Library of Congress Control Number: 2019903553

TEACH Services, Inc.
PUBLISHING
www.TEACHServices.com • (800) 367-1844

TABLE OF CONTENTS

Foreword iv
Preface v
Introduction vi
Chapter 1—True Justification 1
Chapter 2—Bible Sanctification 14
Chapter 3—Living a Spiritual Life 31
Chapter 4—Battle of the Dark Realm 47
Chapter 5—The Journey of Recovery 69
Chapter 6—The Christian Armor 87
Chapter 7—Prevailing Prayer 93
Chapter 8—Battle in the Realm of Prayer 107
Chapter 9—Angels and Demons 121
Chapter 10—The Final Revival 138

FOREWORD

Having read this unique work, *Abiding in the Supernatural*, I'm inspired and challenged by the insights and fresh interpretations of the Scriptures regarding justification, sanctification, living a spiritual life, prayer, and a host of other topics. From the perspective of a church leader with a passion for firm biblical worship and godliness, I affirm that Chinedu Daniel Obasi presents in this book a passionately upbeat picture of true revival, not just one that is emotional and hypocritical, but one that integrates true godliness with sound biblical teachings.

In these few pages, he has explained his stand on revival in a way different from what prevails in Christendom today. He brings out the difference between primitive godliness and our modern false revivals. Today, God's church needs the power of the Pentecost again. Christians need power to live as Jesus lived, win the war against sin, blast through thick walls of selfishness, indifference, and hostility, reach and change human hearts, see committed rebels changed into loyal sons and daughters of God, and finish the work of taking God's final warning to the entire sin-scarred world.

Every Christian who feels impelled to find a deeper dimension of godly living should not only read this book but study it prayerfully and apply its principles to one's life. Shalom!

Pastor Okechukwu Mbaeri
Executive Secretary, Imo Conference
Former Publishing Director, Eastern Nigerian Union of
Seventh-day Adventists

PREFACE

The Christian life is one of warfare. We are called to be good soldiers of the Lord Jesus Christ and fight a good faith of faith. The reason why the Christian life is warfare is that we have a terrible enemy who seeks to destroy us. That enemy is Satan. The Bible warns us, "Be sober, be vigilant; because your adversary the devil, as a roaring lion, walketh about, and seeking whom he may devour" (1 Peter 5:8).

In spite of knowing the verses in the Bible that warn of Satan's attack on the church, Christians today still find it very difficult to accept the fact that there is a battle going on around them for their souls. It is in the light of these clear statements of the Scriptures that this book has been written. Every Christian is a watch person and therefore duty-bound to warn the world and those within one's sphere of the dangers surrounding them.

We are in the era of the supernatural. God wants us to experience the supernatural. We are designed for it. God initially put significant power into the hands of humanity, but they lost it at the fall. Now He has put the power in Christ. He has laid it up in His own Son. It is the believer's privilege to accept and walk into His presence and abide in this atmosphere of glory. May God, therefore, help those who read these pages to heed the warnings and be a channel of light in Jesus. Amen!

CHINEDU DANIEL OBASI

INTRODUCTION

It is with great soberness I write this book as God has impressed me. Dear friend, God's great desire for you is not only to make you holy, but also guide you by His Holy Spirit. He wants all things to go well with you. He is pleased when you are making steady progress in every aspect of your life.

However, there are formidable barriers the enemy puts in the way of your progress. Unless these are removed and destroyed, progress is effectively hindered. How to deal with these barriers in your life once and for all is the subject of this book. If you faithfully read and apply the contents of this book, you will not remain the same again.

From passage to passage and page to page, you will uncover the elaborate, infallible design and counsel of the Lord concerning you. I truly believe you will find this book not only interesting but very inspiring!

Chapter 1

TRUE JUSTIFICATION

How is a person forgiven? How is one justified before God? Many hearts today are earnestly longing for an answer to these very relevant questions.

Everywhere there are hearts crying out for something which they have not. They long for a power that will give them mastery over sin, a power that will deliver them from the bondage of evil, a power that will give health and life and peace. Many who once knew the power of God's word have dwelt where there is no recognition of God, and they long for the divine presence. (White, *Ministry of Healing*, p. 143)

> *How is a person forgiven? How is one justified before God? Many hearts today are earnestly longing for an answer to these very relevant questions*

Related questions on the lips of many today include how can a soul be made righteous? How can one live the life of Christ and bear His likeness? How can one be clothed with His righteousness? How can one obtain God's justification? These bring us to a more overarching question.

What Is Justification?

Justification is pardon. Who does the pardoning? It is God who does the pardoning. Who needs the pardon? It is the sinner who needs God's pardon. Pardon or justification is God's judicious verdict pronounced on a repentant sinner. "Pardon and justification are one and the same thing" (White 1956, p. 1070).

A sinner is a person who commits sin. "All unrighteousness is sin" (1 John 5:17). "Whosoever committeth sin transgresseth also the law: for sin is the transgression of the law" (3:4). "When man transgresses he is under the condemnation of the law, and it becomes to him a yoke of bondage" (White 1952, p. 250).

Therefore, according to the transitive property, in which two things that are equal to the same thing are equal to each other, we have unrighteousness = transgression of the law. Inversely, righteousness = obedience to the law. The perishing sinner may say, "I am a lost sinner," but Christ came to seek and save those who are lost. He says, **"I came not to call the righteous, but sinners to repentance"** (Matt. 9:13, WEB).

Christ and Grace Alone

How can a sinner obtain God's justification? For centuries, hearts have cried out and longed, not only for knowledge, but also the power that will give them mastery over sin. Many have asked, "How shall I be just with God? How shall I be made righteous?"

Jesus says, "…He that abideth in me, and I in him, the same bringeth forth much fruit: for without me ye can do nothing" (John 15:5). Speaking of Jesus, Peter says, "Neither is there salvation in any other: for there is none other name under heaven given among men, whereby we must be saved" (Acts 4:12).

The wiseman, Solomon, wrote, "The name of the LORD [is] a strong tower: the righteous runneth into it, and is safe" (Prov. 18:10).

It is only through Christ we can be made just. It is only through His saving grace we can be brought into harmony with God and with holiness. Jesus says,

> Except a man be born again … That which is born of the flesh is flesh; and that which is born of the Spirit is spirit. Marvel not that I said unto thee, Ye must be born again. The wind bloweth where it listeth, and thou hearest the sound thereof, but canst not tell whence it cometh, and whither it goeth: so is every one that is born of the Spirit. (John 3:3, 6–8)

Unless a man shall receive a new heart, desires, purposes, and motives—a power working from within, a new life from above—there can be no real change from sin to holiness. In other words, until there's a change from old nature to new, there can be no progress.

For the Bible says, "The natural man receiveth not the things of the Spirit of God: for they are foolishness unto him: neither can he know [them], because they are spiritually discerned" (1 Cor. 2:14). A natural man is powerless and cannot of himself escape from the pit of sin into which he has sunken. His heart is evil, and he cannot change it. In Job we read, "Who can bring a clean thing out of an unclean? Not one" (Job 14:4).

Paul also reiterates this thought: "The carnal mind is enmity against God: for it is not subject to the law of God, neither indeed can be" (Rom. 8:7).

Friends, many are the figures by which the Spirit of God has sought to illustrate this wonderful truth, and make it plain to souls that long to be freed from the burden of guilt, who are at the same time yearning for that purity, the righteousness, to which in themselves they are powerless to attain. It is only through Christ we can be justified. So then, what is the first step in a person receiving justification and forgiveness?

Peter says, "Repent ye therefore, and be converted, that your sins may be blotted out" (Acts 3:19). Peter listed repentance as the prerequisite. It will interest you to know that repentance is placed as the first step and what does it entail? Repentance includes sorrow for sin and a turning away from it (White 1892, p. 23).

However, many are confused.

> They think that they cannot come to Christ unless they first repent, and that repentance prepares for the forgiveness of their sins. It is true that repentance does precede the forgiveness of sins; for it is only the broken and contrite heart that will feel the need of a Saviour. But must the sinner wait till he has repented before he can come to Jesus? Is repentance to be made an obstacle between the sinner and the Saviour? (White 1892, p. 26)

The Bible does not teach that the sinner must repent before he can heed the invitation of Christ: "Come unto Me, all ye that labor and are heavy-laden, and I will give you rest" (Matt. 11:28). It is the virtue that goes forth from Christ that leads to genuine repentance. Peter made the matter clear in his statement to the Jews when he said, "Him hath God exalted with His right hand to be a Prince and a Saviour, for to give repentance to Israel, and forgiveness of sins" (Acts 5:31).

We cannot repent without the Spirit of Christ to awaken the conscience. Yes, His grace alone can quicken the lifeless faculties of the soul, and attract it to God … to holiness.

The second step in receiving justification and pardon is one confessing personal sin (see Luke 18:13, 14; 1 John 1:9). "By faith he [the penitent] can bring to God the merits of Christ, and the Lord places the obedience of His Son to the sinner's account. Christ's righteousness is accepted in place of man's failure, and God receives, pardons, justifies, the repentant, believing soul, treats him as though he were righteous, and loves him as He loves his Son" (White 1958, p. 367).

As we stated earlier, pardon and justification are the same. Through faith, the believer passes from the position of a rebel, a child of sin and Satan, to the position of a loyal subject of Christ Jesus, not because of inherent goodness, but because Christ receives the believer as His child by adoption. Sinners receive forgiveness for their sins because these sins are borne by His Substitute. The Lord speaks to His heavenly Father, saying: "'This is my child. I reprieve him from the condemnation of death, giving him my life insurance policy—eternal life—because I have taken his place and have suffered for his sins. He is even My beloved son.' Thus man, pardoned, and clothed with the beautiful garments of Christ's righteousness, stands faultless before God" (White 1956, p. 1070).

"The believing sinner is pronounced innocent, while the guilt is placed on Christ. The righteousness of Christ is placed on the debtor's account, and against his name on the balance sheet is written: Pardoned. Eternal Life" (White 1952, p. 273). God's words have shown that it's only through Christ that we can be made just and brought into harmony with God. Yes, Jesus "was delivered for our offences, and was raised again for our justification" (Rom. 4:25). "In him was life; and the life was the light of men" (John 1:4).

While justification is wholly of Christ, through His grace and by His faith, this wonderful truth has been perverted. Evangelicals have taken this truth to mean that no change takes place when we are justified. However, this view defies the very meaning of the word "justified." The common Greek word translated "justified" is *dikaioo*. The common word translated "righteous" is *dikaios*. In the English language, "justified" and righteous" look so different from each other that we may not always make the connection.

According to *Strong's Concordance*, *dikaios* may be translated "just," as well as "righteous," and *dikaioo* may be translated "righteous," as well as "justified." In one of the most important texts in Scripture, it is significant to note the Greek usage: **"…and he that is righteous [***dikaios***], let him be righteous [***dikaioo***] still"** (Rev 22:11). In the original, both the words "righteous" and "justified" are used in this critical text. Both are verbs, effective aorist, stressing the accomplishment of the action (to be declared righteous; to be justified).

How Can We Come to Christ?

The Scripture says, "Behold, I stand at the door, and knock: if any man hear my voice, and open the door, I will come in to him, and will sup with him, and he with me" (Rev. 3:20). As Christ knocks at the door of our hearts, all that is required of us is to open up our hearts so He can enter. "We are to divest ourselves of everything that separates our souls from him. When this is done, we shall see of the salvation of God" ("The Necessity of Receiving the Holy Spirit," *The Signs of the Times*, August 1, 1892).

> I saw that many had so much rubbish piled up at the door of their heart that they could not get the door open. Some have difficulties between themselves and their brethren to remove. Others have evil tempers, selfish covetousness, to remove, before they can open the door. Others have rolled the world before the door of their heart, which bars the door. All this rubbish must be taken away from the door, and then can they open the door, and welcome the Saviour in. (White, *Spiritual Gifts*, vol. 4b, p. 28)

God's pardon is unmerited favor; we do not in any way merit His goodness. It is while we are yet sinners, weighed down heavily by the load of sin, with guilt looming like a lofty mountain upon our souls and the burden of iniquity poised to fall and crush us, that God's saving grace stretched its hands to us. "Not by works of righteousness which we have done, but according to his mercy he saved us, by the washing of regeneration, and renewing of the Holy Ghost" (Titus 3:5). "By grace are ye saved through faith; and that not of yourselves: *it is* the gift of God" (Eph. 2:8)

> The thought that the righteousness of Christ is imputed to us, not because of any merit on our part, but as a free gift from God, is a precious thought. The enemy of God and man is not willing that this truth should be clearly presented; for he knows that if the people receive it fully, his power will be broken. If he can control minds so that doubt and unbelief and darkness shall compose the experience of those who claim to be the children of God, he can overcome them with temptation. (White, *Gospel Workers*, p. 161)

Speaking about repentance, "It is Christ's virtue that makes repentance sincere and genuine. It has been stated that him whom Christ pardons He first makes penitent. Peter declares the source of repentance when he says, 'Him hath God exalted with His right hand to be a Prince and a Saviour, for to give repentance to Israel, and forgiveness of sins'" ("Obedience the Fruit of Union with Christ," *The Review and Herald*, September 3, 1901).

It is God who draws us to Himself, and He alone can give us true repentance. His offer is free, so if we believe that such a gift can save us, that indeed is faith. Speaking about this faith, Paul wrote, "And be found in him, not having mine own righteousness, which is of the law, but that which is through the faith of Christ, the righteousness which is of God by faith" (Phil. 3:9).

Essential Christian Virtue

Faith is the hand by which we stretch out to receive God's justification. In other words, it is by faith and not by works that we are justified before God. What is faith? "Faith is the substance of things hoped for, the evidence of things not seen" (Heb. 11:1). Here we see faith described in two distinct forms. It is the substance (or solid base) of what one has as a hope, and the evidence (or assurance) of things not visible to the eyes, but which one is persuaded are real.

Mankind, in its fallen sinful state, possesses no genuine faith in God. Its "faith" is nothing but presumption. Describing what humanity's faith looks like before God, the Bible says, "Thou believest that there is one God; thou doest well: the devils also believe, and tremble" (James 2:19). A mere assent to truth is not faith; otherwise, such faith is not different from that of the devil, who believes in God and trembles, but in action is not submissive to His will and law. The Bible calls this presumption.

Presumption is Satan's counterfeit of faith. "Faith claims God's promises and brings forth fruit in obedience. Presumption also claims the promises but uses them as Satan did, to excuse transgression" (White 1977, p. 534). Inasmuch as the path of presumption lies close beside the path of perfect faith and confidence in God, the psalmist's prayer is "Keep back thy servant also from presumptuous sins; let them not have dominion over me: then shall I be upright, and I shall be innocent from the great transgression" (Ps. 19:13).

It is only the person who has true faith who is secure against presumption. However, in reality, genuine faith is in no sense allied to presumption. It is a gift from above. Faith is an essential part of the Christian life. On the divine ladder of Christian experience, there are four levels of faith which, like a wheel, carries us along the road of justification and sanctification to the final heights of victory (glorification). While God has given every person some "measure of faith," His great design is that we shall all grow from "faith to faith" (Rom. 12:3; 1:17). There are four levels of faith: faith in God, faith in His Word, faith in Christ, and the faith of Christ.

In the first level of faith spoken of in Mark 11:22, we are admonished to "Have faith in God." Why is it necessary to have such faith? The Bible says, "But without faith *it is* impossible to please *him* (Heb. 11:6). Here we understand that without a belief in the existence of God, our spiritual life will be unfruitful. What is required besides a belief in the existence of

God? "For he that cometh to God must believe that he is, and *that* he is a rewarder of them that diligently seek him."

Faith in God is the first step in our spiritual walk. "For whatsoever *is* not of faith is sin" (Rom. 14:23). This is a point at which God, through His goodness in the affairs of our daily lives, awakens affection for the heavenly and not only redirecting our minds to the love of God but also establishing our confidence in Him.

Faith in His Word is the second level of faith. What is the basis of this faith? "So then faith *cometh* by hearing, and hearing by the word of God" (Rom. 10:17). When we anchor ourselves on God and dwell on His Word, our faith grows day by day. Can the gospel be profitable without faith? "For unto us was the gospel preached, as well as unto them: but the word preached did not profit them, not being mixed with faith in them that heard *it*" (Heb. 4:2).

Without faith, the gospel cannot be profitable. What relation does faith have with knowledge? "Through faith we understand that the worlds were framed by the word of God, so that things which are seen were not made of things which do appear" (11:3). "The Bible, and the Bible alone, communicates a correct knowledge of the character of God and his will concerning us. The duty and the destiny of man are defined in its pages. The conditions on which we may hope for eternal life are explicitly stated, and the doom of those who neglect so great a salvation is foretold in the most forcible language" ("The Faith That Will Stand the Test," *The Review and Herald*, January 10, 1888).

> *The Word of God offers spiritual liberty and enlightenment to those who seek for it earnestly*

The Word of God offers spiritual liberty and enlightenment to those who seek for it earnestly. Those who accept the promises of God and act on them with living faith will have the light of heaven in their lives. They will drink of the fountain of life and lead others to the waters that have refreshed their own souls.

Regarding the third level of faith, God's Word says, "For ye are all the children of God by faith in Christ Jesus" (Gal. 3:26). It is by this third level, faith in Christ, that we are welcomed into the family of God and hence expected to "walk by faith, not by sight" (2 Cor. 5:7). In his letter to Timothy, Paul spoke about the deacons obtaining a high standing through faith in Christ. "For they that have used the office of a deacon well purchase to themselves a good degree, and great boldness in the faith which is in Christ Jesus" (1 Tim. 3:13).

To believe in Jesus is to have faith in Jesus. A nominal faith in Christ, which accepts Him merely as the Savior of the world, can never bring healing to the soul. The faith that is unto salvation is not a mere intellectual assent to the truth. The only faith that will benefit us is that which embraces Him as a personal Savior and appropriates His merits to ourselves. This is the kind of faith we shall look at next.

The faith of Christ is the fourth level of faith. Let me illustrate the difference. I have faith in brother Dan; I believe in him; he is a good man, honest and straightforward. I can depend on him. However, that is different from saying that I have the faith of brother Dan. To have the faith of Jesus is more than merely having faith in Jesus. It is to have the same kind of faith that He had, And Jesus did have faith. See Him healing the sick and raising the dead. The faith He had is to be ours.

The faith of Christ is the highest peak in the ladder of faith. This is the complete work of God's divine grace in us, making our faith perfect. This is the fulfilled work of His refining process of our faith unto His likeness. By this faith, we are justified. "Knowing that a man is not justified by the works of the law, but by the faith of Jesus Christ, even we have believed in Jesus Christ, that we might be justified by the faith of Christ" (Gal. 2:16).

To believe in Jesus is to have faith in Jesus. From the above text, we see that no one can have the faith of Jesus if he or she had not first believed in Jesus. I am indeed not speaking lightly of faith in Jesus, which is the third step, but there is a step still higher than that which we must take, and that is the faith of Christ. Speaking about this faith, Paul wrote, "And be found in him, not having mine own righteousness, which is of the law, but that which is through the faith of Christ, the righteousness which is of God by faith" (Phil. 3:9).

Such faith is an amazing gift and one of the fruits of the Holy Spirit. In this beautiful word of inspiration, we read, "But the fruit of the Spirit is love, joy, peace, longsuffering, gentleness, goodness, faith" (Gal. 5: 22). It is planted in us to draw us to God. With what, therefore, is the faith of Jesus joined? "Here is the patience of the saints: here *are* they that keep the commandments of God and the faith of Jesus" (Rev. 14:12).

Faith and Obedience

Simple faith and obedience go hand in hand. When we believe that God's gift can save us, this is faith, and if afterward we believed and yet did not step forward and practically accept the offer, that faith then becomes dead. Your faith without action is of no value. How is faith brought to perfection? "Seest thou how faith wrought with his works, and by works was faith made perfect" (James 2:22).

"To make God's grace our own, we must act our part. The Lord does not propose to perform for us either the willing or the doing. His grace is given to work in us to will and to do, but never as a substitute for our effort. Our souls are to be aroused to cooperate. The Holy Spirit works in us, that we may work out our own salvation" (White 1973, p. 111).

"The part man is required to sustain is immeasurably small, yet in the plan of God it is just that part that is needed to make the work a success" (White 1990, p. 113).

The following is an outline of how we can cooperate with God:

S/N	GOD'S PART	S/N	MANKIND'S PART
1	He will draw you through His Spirit.	1	Do not resist His drawing.
2	He will convict you of sin, righteousness, and judgment.	2	Acknowledge your guilt and need of His righteousness.
3	He will give you repentance.	3	Confess and forsake your sins and give Him your heart.
4	He will forgive, cleanse, regenerate, and free you to live the sanctified life.	4	Believe and accept.
5	He will live in you and empower you.	5	Live by faith and bear much fruit.
6	He will make a way of escape when you are tempted.	6	Take God's way of escape and submit to Him.
7	He will be your Advocate if you fall.	7	Repent and turn back to Him.

It is by our cooperation with God in working out our salvation that the following inspired words apply: "[I]f the wicked turn from his wickedness, and do that which is lawful and right, he shall live thereby" (Ezek. 33:19). Isaiah added, "Let the wicked forsake his way, and the unrighteous man his thoughts: and let him return unto the LORD, and he will have mercy upon him; and to our God, for he will abundantly pardon" (55:7).

Our cooperation is needed before we can be saved. Faith is an intangible thing and cannot ordinarily be seen with physical eyes. It is only our actions that confirm that we have faith. Therefore, the only way faith is shown to be present is by the work it produces. When James was explaining this, he said, "I will show thee my faith by my works" (2:18). The faith which justifies is the faith which works. "For not the hearers of the law *are* just before God, but the doers of the law shall be justified" (Rom. 2:13).

In Genesis, we read about Abraham. "And [God] said, Take now thy son, thine only *son* Isaac, whom thou lovest, and get thee into the land of Moriah; and offer him there for a burnt offering upon one of the mountains which I will tell thee of" (Genesis 22:2). Abraham undertook at once to obey. James rhetorically asked, "Was not Abraham our father justified by works, when he had offered Isaac his son upon the altar" (2:21).

The account of Abraham's active willingness to sacrifice Isaac is the best illustration of faith and work. How did Abraham offer up Isaac? The Bible says, "By faith Abraham, when he was tried, offered up Isaac: and he that had received the promises offered up his only begotten *son*. Of whom it was said, That in Isaac shall thy seed be called: Accounting that God *was* able to raise *him* up, even from the dead; from whence also he received him in a figure" (Heb. 11:17–19).

These verses imply that Abraham by faith gave Isaac up to die; he saw him as dead, but by faith, he looked beyond death and saw his resurrection. This willingness to obey and sacrifice his son unfolded in his heart, which only God knew. The intangible needs to be made tangible through physical action—work.

When James clearly stated that Abraham offered Isaac as a sacrifice to God upon the altar, he was speaking not only concerning his intention to present his son in obedience to what he deciphered to be the will of God, but also physically taking him to Mount Moriah and attempting to stab and kill him. Here is faith practically displayed. Abraham so trusted God that he was not afraid to sacrifice Isaac. Those who say and don't do are not people of faith. The obedience which is pleasing to God is the fruit of the working of His power, being fully assured that what He has promised He can perform. This is the faith which is reckoned for righteousness.

The truth in this whole episode is that both justification and sanctification are combined. How does Abraham's experience show that justification and sanctification are inseparable? "By faith Abraham, when he was called to go out into a place which he should after receive for an inheritance, obeyed; and he went out, not knowing whither he went" (Heb 11:8). He heard the voice of God, believed it to be certainly from God, obeyed first in his heart through his acceptance, and practically confirmed it by the action he took when he physically moved out as the Lord commanded him.

The Voice of God

"And thine ears shall hear a word behind thee, saying, This *is* the way, walk ye in it, when ye turn to the right hand, and when ye turn to the left" (Isa. 30:21).

"When God told [Abraham] to offer his son as a sacrifice it was the same voice that had spoken telling him to leave his country and go into a land which God would show him" (White 1980, p. 195).

"Abraham obeyed my voice, and kept my charge, my commandments, my statutes, and my laws" (Gen. 26:5).

He diligently hearkened to the inner voice of God's Spirit and submissively obeyed right in his heart before taking physical action. Do you think it was only by his physical conduct that he was counted righteous? No, of course not! In the beautiful words of the psalmist we read, "I delight to do thy will, O my God: yea, thy law *is* within my heart" (40:8).

The law written in the heart means it has become the center of the thoughts. Thus, confirming that Abraham's obedience was not just mere outward compliance, but the service that flowed from the heart out of love, "Our obedience must be heart-service…. We may not be able to see the path before us, but we shall go forward in obedience, knowing that all issues and results are to be left with God" ("The Blessing of Obedience," *The Signs of the Times*, January 25, 1899).

We need to realize that no real change can ever take place in a human life tangibly unless it begins in the heart. "The heart renewed by the Holy Spirit will bring forth 'the fruits of the Spirit.' Through the grace of Christ we shall live in obedience to the law of God written upon our hearts. Having the Spirit of Christ, we shall walk even as He walked" (White 1991, p. 206).

"For as many as are led by the Spirit of God, they are the sons of God. For ye have not received the spirit of bondage again to fear; but ye have received the Spirit of adoption, whereby we cry, Abba, Father. The Spirit itself beareth witness with our spirit, that we are the children of God" (Rom. 8:14–16). By this Abraham was justified through the gift of faith and righteousness in the Holy Spirit. He was counted righteous. "In order for man to be justified by faith, faith must reach a point where it will control the affections and impulses of the heart; and it is by obedience that faith itself is made perfect" (White 1979, p. 100).

Just as obedience begins in the heart, so does disobedience. The Bible says, "But I say unto you, That whosoever looketh on a woman to lust after her hath committed adultery with her already in his heart" (Matt. 5:28). Just as sin is committed in the heart, so righteousness and good works first take place in the heart. So far in our study, we saw that faith is a gift from God. Abraham's faith was a gift from God; the works of his faith were not self-motivated works, but rather God in Christ working in him. Therefore, "Keep thy heart with all diligence; for out of it *are* the issues of life" (Prov. 4:23).

Abraham is a type of all believers. The Old Testament account of Abraham is the basis of the New Testament teaching of the atonement, the sacrificial offering of the sin of mankind. Jesus said, "Your father Abraham rejoiced to see my day: and he saw *it*, and was glad" (John 8:56). In God's Word Abraham is set forth as a model. The same way he was justified by God through faith, so shall we all be justified. "And the scripture, foreseeing that God would justify the heathen through faith, preached before the gospel unto Abraham, *saying*, In thee shall all nations be blessed" (Gal. 3:8).

The Thief on the Cross

"And he said unto Jesus, Lord, remember me when thou comest into thy kingdom. And Jesus said unto him, Verily I say unto thee, today shalt thou be with me in paradise" (Luke 23:42, 43). The poor criminal had been led astray by evil associations, and by his perverse way of life he had plunged deeper and deeper into sin until he was arrested, tried as a criminal, and condemned to die on the cross. While on the cross dying as a common criminal, this thief pleaded for mercy. What a faith he had!

"Divinity flashes through humanity. From those pale and quivering lips the words are distinctly heard by the dying penitent and by all surrounding the cross, 'Verily I say unto thee today, Thou shalt be with Me in paradise'" ("Our Sacrifice," *The Signs of the Times*, December 8, 1898).

What if he had not pleaded? He wouldn't have been saved. It did not take the thief many days to obtain pardon; he received pardon and was instantly eligible for heaven. This indeed is God's assurance of His immutable love. If we confess our sins to Him, He is faithful and just to forgive us of our sins and cleanse us from all our unrighteousness instantly.

No amount of good works can erase sins committed in the past. The old rugged cross on Calvary is an eternal memorial of the price God was willing to pay for our sins. And this is justification. It is the outflow of God's redeeming love that transforms the heart. David had the true conception of God's justification when he prayed, "Create in me a clean heart, O God; and renew a right spirit within me" (Ps. 51:10).

It is true that today many souls are kept from obeying the truth or living a victorious life because of the confusion of ideas and not knowing how to surrender their wills and minds to Jesus. They want special instructions on how to become Christians. Additionally, some of those who come to God by repentance and confession have often failed to believe that they've been fully cleansed from all their sins. They still doubt if they are now truly cleansed from all their sins and pardoned.

These people fail to claim by faith God's promises or see that Jesus is an ever-present Savior to whom they can commit the keeping of their souls. While they think they are committing themselves to God, there is a great deal of self-dependence. These are conscientious souls who trust partly to God and partly to themselves.

Friends, no one can ever be sanctified while sin is cherished in the heart. "Until we turn away from it in heart, there will be no real change in the life" (White 1970, p. 63). For real change to take place in our lives, "The sinner must go to Christ in order that he may be enabled to repent. It is the virtue that goes forth from Jesus which strengthens the purposes of the heart to turn away from sin and to cleave to that which is truth" ("Obedience the Fruit of Union with Christ," The Review and Herald, September 3, 1901).

When sinners see Jesus lifted on the cross, dying that they might not perish but have everlasting life, they realize something of the enormity of sin and long for pardon for all their transgressions and the favor of God. As the Holy Spirit impresses their minds, they pray most earnestly and believe that if they ask, they shall receive. They present the promise and rejoice in the pardoning love of God, and their sincerity in the service of God and reality of their conversion are made manifest by the vigor of their endeavor to obey all of God's commandments. The soul who has found the Lord will renounce every wicked work, cease to do evil, and learn to do well because Christ is formed within, the hope of glory.

CHAPTER 2

BIBLE SANCTIFICATION

What is the definition of Christian sanctification? The word "sanctification" is related to the word "saint." Both have to do with holiness. Which inspired prayer sets the standard for the Christian experience? "And the very God of peace sanctify you wholly; and *I pray God* your whole spirit and soul and body be preserved blameless unto the coming of our Lord Jesus Christ" (1 Thess. 5:23).

To sanctify something is to set it apart for special use; to sanctify a person is to make that person holy. The Bible clearly teaches what sanctification is and how it is to be attained. God's perfect will for us is to be holy in body, spirit, and soul. The Savior prayed for His disciples. "Sanctify them through thy truth: thy word is truth" (John 17:17).

> *It is by God's Word that we are sanctified, although not just by mere confession of it, but by practically living a life of willing obedience to it. Then our lives are energized by the power of the Holy Spirit*

It is by God's Word that we are sanctified, although not just by mere confession of it, but by practically living a life of willing obedience to it. Then our lives are energized by the power of the Holy Spirit. It is on this basis that Paul wrote that we are "sanctified by the Holy Ghost" (Rom. 15:16).

What is the work of the Holy Spirit? Jesus told His disciples, "When he, the Spirit of truth, is come, he will guide you into all truth" (John 16:13). The psalmist said, "Thy law is the truth." Since the law of God is "holy, and just, and good," a transcript of divine perfection, it follows that a character formed by obedience to that law will be holy.

Christ is a perfect example of such a character. He said, "I have kept my Father's commandments" (John 15:10). "I do always those things that please him" (8:29). What is righteousness? Righteousness is primarily right-being. This leads to right-doing. The Bible says, "Little children, let no man deceive you: he that doeth righteousness is righteous, even as he is righteous" (1 John 3:7).

We do righteousness. It is a way of living. There are three kinds of righteousness identified in God's Word: human righteousness (righteousness of the law), imputed righteousness (justification) and imparted righteousness (sanctification). "And be found in him, not having mine own righteousness, which is of the law, but that which is through the faith of Christ, the righteousness which is of God by faith" (Phil. 3:9).

There's human righteousness and God's righteousness. His pardon includes an instant deposit of His righteousness through the faith of Christ into the sinner's account. He imputes (credits) the obedience and righteousness of His Son to us. In justification, He credits the believer with the moral perfection of His own dear Son, and we receive it through faith.

In sanctification, that which was credited to us and we accept by faith, we now make ours through the daily representation of Christ's life in our lives. By daily victory and good standing with the Lord, we become a set apart for God from the world while in the world.

Therefore, the followers of Christ are to become like Him by the grace of God that forms characters in harmony with the principles of His holy law. Our lives are to be guided by His ten moral codes.

God's Ten Moral Codes

1. "Thou shalt have no other gods before me" (Ex. 20:3).

    Whatever we cherish that tends to lessen our love for God or to interfere with the service due Him, of that do we make a god. (White 1955, p. 56)

2. "Thou shalt not make unto thee any graven image, or any likeness *of anything* that *is* in heaven above, or that *is* in the earth beneath, or that *is* in the water under the earth: Thou shalt not bow down thyself to them, nor serve them" (vs. 4–6.).

    The second commandment forbids the worship of the true God by images or similitudes.... The mind, turned away from the infinite perfection of Jehovah, would be attracted to the creature rather than to the Creator. (Ibid., p. 57)

3. "Thou shalt not take the name of the LORD thy God in vain; for the LORD will not hold him guiltless that taketh his name in vain" (v. 7).

   This commandment not only prohibits false oaths and common swearing, but it forbids us to use the name of God in a light or careless manner, without regard to its awful significance. By the thoughtless mention of God in common conversation, by appeals to Him in trivial matters, and by the frequent and thoughtless repetition of His name, we dishonor Him. 'Holy and reverend is His name.' All should meditate upon His majesty, His purity and holiness, that the heart may be impressed with a sense of His exalted character; and His holy name should be uttered with reverence and solemnity. Burning words of passion should never be spoken, for in the sight of God and holy angels they are as a species of swearing. (Ibid., p. 58)

4. "Remember the sabbath day, to keep it holy. Six days shalt thou labour, and do all thy work: But the seventh day *is* the sabbath of the LORD thy God... For *in* six days the LORD made heaven and earth, the sea, and all that in them *is*, and rested the seventh day: wherefore the LORD blessed the sabbath day, and hallowed it" (vs. 8–11).

   Pointing to God as the maker of the heavens and the earth, [the Sabbath] distinguishes the true God from all false gods. All who keep the seventh day, signify by this act that they are worshippers of Jehovah [see Rev. 14:6, 7]. Thus the Sabbath is the sign of man's allegiance to God as long as there are any upon the earth to serve Him. (Ibid., p. 59)

5. "Honour thy father and thy mother: that thy days may be long upon the land which the LORD thy God giveth thee" (v. 12).

   The fifth commandment requires the children not only to yield respect, submission, and obedience to their parents, but also to give them love and tenderness, to lighten their cares, to guard their reputation, and to succor and comfort them in old age. (Ibid., p. 60)

6. "Thou shalt not kill" (v. 13).

   All acts of injustice that tend to shorten life; the spirit of hatred and revenge, or the indulgence of any passion that leads to injurious acts toward others, or causes us even to wish them harm (for "whosoever hateth his brother is a murderer"); a selfish neglect of caring for the needy or suffering; all self-indulgence or unnecessary deprivation or excessive labor that tends to injure health--all these are, to a greater or less degree, violations of the sixth commandment. (White 1890, p. 308)

7. "Thou shalt not commit adultery" (v. 14).

   This commandment forbids not only acts of impurity, but sensual thoughts and desires, or any practice that tends to excite them. Purity is demanded not only in the outward life, but in the secret intents and emotions of the heart. Christ, who taught the far-reaching obligation of the law of God, declared the evil thought or look to be as truly sin as is the unlawful deed. (White 1955, p. 62)

8. "Thou shalt not steal" (v. 15).

   Both public and private sins are included in this prohibition. The eighth commandment condemns man-stealing and slave-dealing, and forbids wars of conquest. It condemns theft and robbery. It demands strict integrity in the minutest details of the affairs of life. It forbids overreaching in trade, and requires the payment of just debts or wages. It declares that every attempt to advantage one's self by the ignorance, weakness, or misfortune of another, is registered as fraud in the books of heaven. (Ibid., p. 63).

9. "Thou shalt not bear false witness against thy neighbour" (v. 16).

   False speaking in any matter, every attempt or purpose to deceive our neighbor, is here included. An intention to deceive is what constitutes falsehood. By a glance of the eye, a motion of the hand, an expression of the countenance, a falsehood may be told as effectually as by words. All intentional overstatement, every hint or insinuation calculated to convey an erroneous or exaggerated impression, even the statement of facts in such a manner as to mislead, is falsehood. This precept forbids every effort to injure our neighbor's reputation by misrepresentation or evil surmising, by slander or tale bearing. Even the intentional suppression of truth, by which injury may result to others, is a violation of the ninth commandment. (White 1890, p. 309)

10. "Thou shalt not covet" (v. 17).

    The last commandment condemns covetousness. Every selfish desire, every degree of discontent, every act of overreaching, every selfish gratification works to the strengthening and developing of a character which will destroy the Christlikeness of the human agent, and close the gates of the city of God against him....The tenth commandment strikes at the very root of all sins, prohibiting the selfish desire, from which springs the sinful act. He who in obedience to God's law refrains from indulging even a sinful desire for that which belongs to another, will not be guilty of an act of wrong toward his fellow-creatures. (White 1955, p. 56)

True Consecration

Which inspired prayer sets the standard for Christian experience? "And the very God of peace sanctify you wholly; and *I pray God* your whole spirit and soul and body be preserved blameless unto the coming of our Lord Jesus Christ" (1 Thessalonians 5:23). "The sanctification set forth in the Sacred Scriptures has to do with the entire being—spirit, soul, and body. Here is the true idea of entire consecration. Paul prays that the church at Thessalonica may enjoy this great blessing" (White 1937, p. 7).

How necessary is this experience? "Follow peace with all *men*, and holiness, without which no man shall see the Lord" (Heb. 12:14). Paul's admonition is that we must be peacemakers, aim for perfection, and never lower the standard of righteousness to accommodate inherited and cultivated tendencies to wrongdoing.

Again, he writes to believers, "I beseech you therefore, brethren, by the mercies of God that ye present your bodies a living sacrifice, holy, acceptable unto God" (Rom. 12:1). To do this, all their powers must be preserved in the best possible condition. Every practice that weakens physical or mental strength unfits a person for the service of the Creator. "Only those who are clothed in the garments of His righteousness will be able to endure the glory of His presence when He shall appear with 'power and great glory'" (White 1955, p. 368).

How can it be proved that a person is being sanctified? "Ye shall know them by their fruits. Do men gather grapes of thorns, or figs of thistles? Even so every good tree bringeth forth good fruit; but a corrupt tree bringeth forth evil fruit" (Matt. 7:16–18).

> Self-denial, self-sacrifice, benevolence, kindness, love, patience, fortitude, and Christian trust are the daily fruits borne by those who are truly connected with God. Their acts may not be published to the world, but they themselves are daily wrestling with evil, and gaining precious victories over temptation and wrong. Solemn vows are renewed, and kept through the strength gained by earnest prayer and constant watching thereunto. (White, *The Sanctified Life*, p. 11)

> Sanctification means habitual communion with God. (White, *In Heavenly Places*, p. 129)

> True sanctification means perfect love, perfect obedience, perfect conformity to the will of God. We are to be sanctified to God through obedience to the truth. Our conscience must be purged from dead works to serve the living God. We are not yet perfect; but it is our privilege

to cut away from the entanglements of self and sin, and advance to perfection. Great possibilities, high and holy attainments, are placed within the reach of all. (White, *The Acts of the* Apostles, p. 565)

Early Reformers

The early reformers proclaimed that the gospel is justification alone, thus excluding sanctification from the gospel. However, the Bible denies this very basis of the reformers' view of salvation. Justification and sanctification are strongly "married" together in the Bible. "The righteousness by which we are justified is imputed; the righteousness by which we are sanctified is imparted. The first is our title to heaven, the second is our fitness for heaven" (White 1958, p. 116).

Justification (God's pardon) transforms the heart. Out of the abundance of the heart, through daily conformity with the will of God, our lives are sanctified through obedience. The reformers rejected a gospel consisting of justification and sanctification to contradict Catholicism. And many articulate supporters of reformation theology accuse those who hold the fundamental, biblical concept of a gospel that incorporates both justification and sanctification of placing themselves in the Catholic tradition rather than in the Protestant tradition.

With that said, the fact remains that the Catholic concept of sanctification is different altogether from biblical sanctification. Catholic sanctification is a work-oriented concept that is centered on the seven sacred sacraments:

1. Mass
2. Holy Order
3. Marriage
4. Baptism
5. Penance
6. Confirmation
7. Extreme unction

Catholic sanctification is built upon sacraments, but biblical sanctification is God's perfect work for mankind through the sacrifice and ministry of His Son Jesus Christ. What charge did Jesus bring against the Pharisees? "For laying aside the commandment of God, ye hold the tradition of men, *as* the washing of pots and cups: and many other such like things ye do" (Mark 7:8).

Human tradition is the voice of humanity preserved in the church. To follow the traditions of mankind instead of obeying the commandments of God is to repeat the sins of the past. How highly does God regard obedience to His commandments in the lives of people? "And Samuel said, Hath the LORD *as great* delight in burnt offerings and sacrifices, as in obeying the voice of the LORD? Behold, to obey *is* better than sacrifice, *and* to hearken than the fat of rams" (1 Sam. 15:22).

God values genuine obedience. However, many people have somehow overlooked the fact that the same faith that justifies also sanctifies. In exploring the relationship of justification and sanctification to the cross, almost all Christians accept that we are justified by the blood of Jesus Christ. "Much more then, being now justified by his blood, we shall be saved from wrath through him" (Rom. 5:9).

Elsewhere, Paul reaffirms that we are sanctified through the sacrifice of Christ. "Wherefore Jesus also, that he might sanctify the people with his own blood, suffered without the gate" (Heb. 13:12). "By the which will we are sanctified through the offering of the body of Jesus Christ once *for all*" (10:10).

The Bible is rich in passages that declare that sanctification is God's work. "But we are bound to give thanks alway to God for you, brethren beloved of the Lord, because God hath from the beginning chosen you to salvation through sanctification of the Spirit and belief of the truth" (2 Thess. 2:13).

It is of utmost importance to recognize that blood-bought justification and sanctification do not exist without works of righteousness. What encouragement is extended as an aid in attaining this experience? "For this is the will of God, *even* your sanctification that ye should abstain from fornication" (1 Thess. 4:3).

Bible sanctification is conformity to the will of God, attained by rendering obedience to His law through the faith of Christ. Sanctification includes daily dying to self and continually growing in grace. There can only be one reason for attempting to separate sanctification from the gospel. It is a campaign by Satan to keep men and women in unrighteousness so that they will ultimately be lost.

In the experience of sanctification, what attitude must one assume towards the truth? "But we are bound to give thanks alway to God for you, brethren beloved of the Lord, because God hath from the beginning chosen you to salvation through sanctification of the Spirit and belief of the truth" (2 Thess. 2:13).

There is no question that these words are to apply to us. The object of all the provisions of heaven is the salvation of our souls. It is God's purpose that His people shall be a sanctified, purified, holy people, communicating light to those around them, and by exemplifying the truth in their lives, they shall be praised in the earth. These are the great, transcendent truths that bring mankind to justification and sanctification and prepare God's people for the judgment and fellowship with the holy angels and Jesus Himself throughout eternity.

Catholics and Salvation

The Roman Catholic Church is one of the most powerful institutions on earth. In one way or another, its beliefs hold sway over literally a billion people around the world. What does Catholicism teach about the doctrines of salvation, justification, and sanctification?

Baptism

Baptism is one of the seven sacraments of the Catholic Church. It teaches that when infants are baptized, they are cleansed "from original sin, this privilege removes other sin and its punishment, provides justification in an initial form, provides spiritual rebirth or regeneration, and this sacrament is necessary for salvation" (Ankerberg & Weldon 2004, p. 57).

Infant baptism is not taught anywhere in Scripture. Jesus was in a better position to show an example if indeed it was part of God's divine plan, but He did not. At what age was Christ baptized? "It came to pass, that Jesus also being baptized, and praying, the heaven was opened … himself began to be about thirty years of age" (Luke 1:21, 23).

Why did Christ not show an example if it was God's original plan? What about the 4,000 years before the birth of Christianity? What would have been the fate of those millions of little infants that did not have the privilege of being baptized according to Catholic dogma? Do the sins of parents really affect the heritage of their children? If yes, how?

Well, parents pass on humanity's fallen nature to their children, including their weaknesses, tendencies, and propensities, but this does not in any way make infants sinners at birth, nor are they accounted guilty of anything. Of Jesus, the Bible says, "But when the fulness of the time was come, God sent forth his Son, made of a woman, made under the law" (Gal. 4:4).

> Forasmuch then as the children are partakers of flesh and blood, he also himself likewise took part of the same; that through death he might

> destroy him that had the power of death, that is, the devil… For verily he took not on *him the nature of* angels; but he took on *him* the seed of Abraham. Wherefore in all things it behoved him to be made like unto *his* brethren… For in that he himself hath suffered being tempted, he is able to succour them that are tempted. (Hebrews 2:14, 16–18)

"Though he were a Son, yet learned he obedience by the things which he suffered; And being made perfect, he became the author of eternal salvation unto all them that obey him" (Heb 5:8, 9). Christ bore the same nature as mankind and was not a sinner at birth. God does not hold infants accountable for lawbreaking. No passage of Scripture attests to that, but we are born with a sinful nature. That is why we need to be born again, but not in our infancy.

Shocking is the belief held by those who accept the diabolical error of original sin. "Whosoever committeth sin transgresseth also the law: for sin is the transgression of the law" (1 John 3:4). The Bible did not say sin is inherited, but an act of willful transgression. We are further told, "The soul that sinneth, it shall die. The son shall not bear the iniquity of the father, neither shall the father bear the iniquity of the son: the righteousness of the righteous shall be upon him, and the wickedness of the wicked shall be upon him" (Ezek. 18:20).

Praise God! We are not counted sinners because of our parents' transgressions. We are sinners by choice, for we sinned when we chose to yield to our weaknesses and propensities. Can God forgive and justify the sinner without repentance and confession? Absolutely not! The Bible says, "If we confess our sins, he is faithful and just to forgive us *our* sins, and to cleanse us from all unrighteousness" (1 John 1:9).

Infants can't confess their sins because they don't know anything. God's pardon is only available to those who are sincerely sorry for their sins. Instantly, when God sees this sincere sorrow for sin, there is forgiveness and justification. He treats sinners as if they never sinned.

Confirmation

Confirmation is also one of the seven sacraments of the Catholic Church. It does not happen at the infant stage. The child must first grow to the age of comprehension while being taught the primary tenets of the church's beliefs as documented in the Catechism. Afterward, confirmation takes place, and this, according to the Catholic Church, endows the child with the Holy Spirit in a distinct sense, which leads to an increase of sanctifying grace, as well as other spiritual powers and sealing to the Catholic faith.

Confirmation also gives strength from the Holy Spirit to defend the Catholic faith and avoid temptation.

In this ritual, the church teaches that the broader process of justification begins at this stage because justification cannot start prior to faith, which is defined as "man's assent to revealed (that is, Catholic), truth nor can it occurs before baptism" (Ankerberg & Weldon 2004, p. 58). This idea that a child is to be confirmed after baptism when grown is not biblical.

> Now when the apostles which were at Jerusalem heard that Samaria had received the word of God, they sent unto them Peter and John: Who, when they were come down, prayed for them, that they might receive the Holy Ghost: (For as yet he was fallen upon none of them: only they were baptized in the name of the Lord Jesus.) Then laid they *their* hands on them, and they received the Holy Ghost. (Acts 8:14–17)

When they heard *this*, they were baptized in the name of the Lord Jesus. And when Paul had laid *his* hands upon them, the Holy Ghost came on them; and they spake with tongues, and prophesied. (Acts 19:5, 6)

Catholicism teaches that the people of Samaria and Ephesus were baptized in Christ, but did not receive the fullness of the Spirit until they were confirmed by the elders and Paul, respectively. For that reason, confirmation is an institution of Jesus Christ within His "bride," the Catholic Church, to further strengthen those who have reached adulthood. However, the truth is that these Samaritans were not baptized as infants, and the laying on of hands was not confirmation. In fact, the apostles who received the Holy Spirit on the day of Pentecost were not baptized as infants.

Another evidence proving the account of confirmation to be false is the case of Cornelius and Peter. We are told how Peter met Cornelius, a Gentile who was never baptized at any time. While Peter was yet speaking, they received the Holy Spirit. Now look at what the Bible says:

> While Peter yet spake these words, the Holy Ghost fell on all them which heard the word. And they of the circumcision which believed were astonished, as many as came with Peter, because that on the Gentiles also was poured out the gift of the Holy Ghost. For they heard them speak with tongues, and magnify God. Then answered Peter, Can any man forbid water, that these should not be baptized, which have received the Holy Ghost as well as we? And he commanded them to be baptized in the name of the Lord. Then prayed they him to tarry certain days. (Acts 10:44–48)

If we go according to Catholic teaching, they were confirmed even before they were baptized. How could God confirm those who were not baptized if such a practice was from Him? The fact remains that the Bible does not in any way teach confirmation at all. It is silent on the matter.

We are only told that "The Spirit itself beareth witness with our spirit, that we are the children of God" (Rom. 8:16).

> *When we accept Christ as Lord and Savior, the Holy Spirit takes up residence in our hearts and gives us the assurance that He is present and we belong to Him*

When we accept Christ as Lord and Savior, the Holy Spirit takes up residence in our hearts and gives us the assurance that He is present and we belong to Him. He also teaches and explains spiritual things to us. "Which things also we speak, not in the words which man's wisdom teacheth, but which the Holy Ghost teacheth; comparing spiritual things with spiritual. But the natural man receiveth not the things of the Spirit of God: for they are foolishness unto him: neither can he know *them*, because they are spiritually discerned" (1 Cor. 2:13, 14).

The idea that in the following Bible verse—"Of the doctrine of baptisms, and of laying on of hands, and of resurrection of the dead, and of eternal judgment" (Heb. 6:2)—Paul giving instruction to the Hebrews about the laying on of hands in reference to confirmation, not ordination, is also false. What Paul meant in the phrase "laying on of hands" was nothing other than ordination.

What Is Penance?

Penance, according to Catholics, is an act of punishment inflicted on oneself as an outward expression of repentance for wrongdoing. It may involve what is known as mortification. The sacrament of penance is designed specifically to deal with sins committed after baptism. Why? Because the grace that is received or infused at baptism can be entirely lost by mortal (deadly) sin. Mortal sin is considered deadly because it destroys the grace of God within a person, making salvation necessary again. A Catholic who commits mortal sin is immediately destined for eternal punishment in hell.

According to Catholic teaching, a new sacrament is necessary to restore an individual to the state of grace first received at baptism. Penance has three parts:

1. **Contrition**: The person must be sorry for his or her sins
2. **Confession**: The person must fully confess each mortal sin to a priest.
3. **Satisfaction**: The person must perform works of piety such as fasting, saying prayers (Rosary), almsgiving, and Eucharist, as well as mortification or self-punishment such as wearing an irritating shirt woven with coarse animal hair, or making a religious pilgrimage to a shrine of Christ, Mary, or dead saints.

Penance (or reconciliation) removes the penalty of sins committed after baptism and confirmation. Mortal, or "deadly," sins are remitted and the "justification" lost by such sins is restored as a continuing process. Penance is a particular act or acts considered as satisfaction offered to God in reparation for sin committed. According to the Catholic Encyclopedia, Jesus Christ Himself instituted the sacrament of penance for "the pardon of sins committed after baptism." Thus, "In the sacrament of penance, the faithful obtain from the mercy of God pardon for their sins against Him... (Paul II, 1995, pp. 466, 467)

The Bible is totally silent on this subject, although the Catholic Douay-Rheims Bible commonly substitutes the word "repent" with "do penance." However, the terms are not related. Repentance is a sorrowful, contrite heart; a feeling of remorse for our sins and a desire and willingness to turn away from them, while penance is self-inflicted pain such as crawling on one's knees or hitting oneself.

Jesus' sacrifice on the cross is sufficient to forgive all our sins. We can't add to it. "Not by works of righteousness which we have done, but according to his mercy he saved us, by the washing of regeneration, and renewing of the Holy Ghost" (Titus 3:5). Everyone will have to look to Jesus for the forgiveness of sins. If people want to perform good deeds because they now see the error of their ways and want to please God, that's good, but this will not achieve forgiveness, for it is free.

What Is an Indulgence?

According to Catholic teaching:

The remission of the temporal punishment due for sins and hence, the satisfaction owed to God for one's sins is called an indulgence. Indulgences granted by the Church may be gained for oneself or for the souls in purgatory. The granting of indulgences is founded upon three doctrines of Catholic faith: the treasury of the merits of the communion of saints, Christ himself, and the Blessed Virgin and the saints. (Ankerberg & John Weldon, *Fast Facts on Roman Catholicism*, p. 77)

Thus, it is a remission before God of the temporal punishment, either here or in purgatory, due to sins, the guilt of which has already been forgiven. While we cannot deny the fact that King David's sins against Bathsheba and Uriah were forgiven, he nevertheless had to suffer the discipline of God for what he had done, as Nathan the prophet declared. However, God's Word did not describe this as an indulgence; that's purely based on Catholic tradition. This is not meant to deny the fact that the Bible teaches that God disciplines believers when they sin. For instance, "I will be his father, and he shall be my son. If he commit iniquity, I will chasten him with the rod of men, and with the stripes of the children of men" (2 Sam. 7:14).

> For whom the Lord loveth he chasteneth, and scourgeth every son whom he receiveth. If ye endure chastening, God dealeth with you as with sons; for what son is he whom the father chasteneth not? But if ye be without chastisement, whereof all are partakers, then are ye bastards, and not sons. Furthermore we have had fathers of our flesh which corrected *us*, and we gave *them* reverence: shall we not much rather be in subjection unto the Father of spirits, and live? For they verily for a few days chastened *us* after their own pleasure; but he for *our* profit, that *we* might be partakers of his holiness. Now no chastening for the present seemeth to be joyous, but grievous: nevertheless afterward it yieldeth the peaceable fruit of righteousness unto them which are exercised thereby. (Hebrews 12:6–11)

Please note that the chastening of the Lord is for backsliding believers who commit iniquity by living in known sin. God employs it to bring them back to faith. With that said, discipline does not occur in purgatory, but while His erring children are living on earth. The Bible says, "This *is* the covenant that I will make with them after those days, saith the Lord, I will put my laws into their hearts, and in their minds will I write them; And their sins and iniquities will I remember no more" (Heb 10:16, 17).

> Again, when I say unto the wicked, Thou shalt surely die; if he turn from his sin, and do that which is lawful and right; *If* the wicked restore the pledge, give again that he had robbed, walk in the statutes of life, without committing iniquity; he shall surely live, he shall not die. None of his sins that he hath committed shall be mentioned unto him: he hath done that which is lawful and right; he shall surely live. (Ezekiel 33:14–16)

"For I will be merciful to their unrighteousness, and their sins and their iniquities will I remember no more" (Heb 8:12). If God will not remember the sins and iniquities of His people after they have been forgiven, and if

He will not mention it to them because He made a covenant with them, then how does one believe He will temporarily punish in purgatory that which He has already forgotten? No punishment whatsoever is owed to God in this life or thereafter once sins have been forgiven and sinners have completely turned from their sinful ways. That is God's promise!

Purgatory

The doctrine of purgatory is integral to the Roman Catholic understanding of redemption. It is the place where the vast majority of professing Roman Catholic Christians go upon their death. The church declares that people who die with any spots, blemishes, impurities, or stains on their souls, instead of going directly to heaven, they must first go to this place of purging, which is this intermediate state between earth and heaven.

Rome makes it clear that purgatory is not hell. It is not a place of the punitive wrath of God, but a place for the corrective wrath of God, as it were, where the sanctifying process is continued through the crucible of fire. A person may be there for two weeks or 200 million years, as long as it takes to become truly, inherently righteous, and once that process is completed, that person can be declared justified by God and released into heaven.

The Bible does not teach that purgatorial suffering is necessary to enter heaven. "For by one offering he hath perfected for ever them that are sanctified." (Heb. 10:14). "For by grace are ye saved through faith; and that not of yourselves: *it is* the gift of God: Not of works, lest any man should boast" (Eph. 2:8, 9).

Catholics believe that purgatory is a place of cleansing in preparation for heaven because they do not recognize that because of Jesus' sacrifice and mediatorial work in the heavenly sanctuary, we are to be forgiven, cleansed, declared righteous, redeemed, reconciled, and sanctified here on earth before death.

Concerning the state of the dead, the Bible says, "For the living know that they shall die: but the dead know not any thing, neither have they any more a reward; for the memory of them is forgotten. Also their love, and their hatred, and their envy, is now perished; neither have they any more a portion for ever in any *thing* that is done under the sun" (Eccles. 9:5, 6). "For in death *there is* no remembrance of thee: in the grave who shall give thee thanks" (Ps. 6:5)? The dead do not know anything, which means they are unconscious, and if that's the case, why would one say they're in purgatory experiencing temporal chastisement?

The Treasury of Merit

In what way does indulgence play a role in releasing a soul undergoing temporal punishment in purgatory? According to Roman Catholic teaching, it is believed that a drop of Christ's blood would contain enough merit to save the whole world. With that said, Christ shed a vast amount of blood as He was crucified. After saving the world with a single drop of blood, the excess, unused blood was stored in God's treasury of merit in heaven. The church also teaches that Mary was sinless. She gained far more merit than what was needed for heaven, so the extra merit she acquired was added to the treasury chest, along with the excess merits of all the saints who again had more than enough merit to enter heaven for themselves.

The Power to Dispense Merit

According to Catholic teaching, the treasury of merit is placed under the charge of the pope, who alone possesses the key and has the power and authority to delegate to anyone the right to dispense merit at their discretion in what is called indulgences. The pope or his delegated representative is believed to have the power to grant indulgences to those who fulfill certain conditions. These indulgences are to provide relief from the temporal punishments of purgatory and are measured in terms of time: hours, days, weeks, months, and years.

Of Jesus, the Bible says, "Neither is there salvation in any other: for there is none other name under heaven given among men, whereby we must be saved" (Acts 4:12). If this is true (and it is), why then are we being led to look to the merits of Mary and the saints? Why look to mere mortals to dispense Christ's merits for our salvation? Do we have other mediators besides Christ? "For *there is* one God, and one mediator between God and men, the man Christ Jesus" (1 Tim. 2:5). "And to Jesus the mediator of the new covenant, and to the blood of sprinkling, that speaketh better things than *that of* Abel" (Heb 12:24). "And for this cause he is the mediator of the New Testament, that by means of death, for the redemption of the transgressions *that were* under the first testament, they which are called might receive the promise of eternal inheritance" (9:15).

The Bible is very clear about Christ and His role in salvation. God has strictly warned us against human tradition. "Howbeit in vain do they worship me, teaching *for* doctrines the commandments of men. For laying aside the commandment of God, ye hold the tradition of men... Full well ye reject the commandment of God, that ye may keep your own tradition.... Making the word of God of none effect through your tradition" (Mark 7:7–9, 13).

Compare Catholic traditions with the Bible, and you'll see they contradict each other. That's why to avoid such embarrassment, the church claims she's above the Scriptures. How can any entity be above God's Word? "The grass withereth, the flower fadeth: but the word of our God shall stand for ever" (Isa. 40:8). "I will worship toward thy holy temple, and praise thy name for thy lovingkindness and for thy truth: for thou hast magnified thy word above all thy name" (Ps. 138:2).

A person's name stands for his or her character and personality. It is the same with God. When He places His word above His name, it means that His name stands as the bedrock. In other words, His name becomes the foundation of His word, and that is His pledge, that His word will be fulfilled. Take for instance when God spoke to Abraham. He swore by Himself. "For when God made promise to Abraham, because he could swear by no greater, he sware by himself, Saying, Surely blessing I will bless thee, and multiplying I will multiply thee" (Heb. 6:13, 14).

How can mere mortals or the imperfect institutions they comprise claim to be above the Word of the Sovereign of the whole universe, attributing infallibility to themselves, alleging to be wiser than God who created them, and arrogating the authority to change God's Word? Is that not blasphemy?

How were the Scriptures given? "All scripture *is* given by inspiration of God" (2 Tim. 3:16). By whom were those who thus spoke for God directed? "For the prophecy came not in old time by the will of man: but holy men of God spake *as they were* moved by the Holy Ghost" (2 Peter 1:21). Who, therefore, spoke through these men? "God, who at sundry times and in divers manners spake in time past unto the fathers by the prophets" (Heb. 1:1).

For what purpose were the Scriptures written? "For whatsoever things were written aforetime were written for our learning, that we through patience and comfort of the scriptures might have hope" (Rom. 15:4). For what is all Scripture profitable? "…doctrine, for reproof, for correction, for instruction in righteousness" (2 Tim. 3:16). How then do Catholics anchor their faith more in the traditions that contradict the pure Word of God, when the Scripture is strictly designed so "That the man of God may be perfect, thoroughly furnished unto all good works" (v. 17).

My dear friends, God's grace is only available to those who not only believe in His Word but are also sincerely sorry for their sins. Instantly, when God sees this sincere sorrow for sin, there is forgiveness and justification, and He treats sinners as if they never sinned. To be born again is not a one-time experience. It is a daily experience. To be renewed in holiness daily should be the goal of every Christian. This is what the new birth is all about. This is justification and sanctification blended together.

CHAPTER 3

LIVING A SPIRITUAL LIFE

The terms "spirituality" and "spiritual life" may appear confusing to some people. From a biblical perspective, what is a spiritual life? Let's look at Peter's description: "Ye also, as lively stones, are built up a spiritual house, an holy priesthood, to offer up spiritual sacrifices, acceptable to God by Jesus Christ" (1 Peter 2:5). Which aspect of us is built spiritually? "This is what we speak, not in words taught us by human wisdom but in words taught by the Spirit, explaining spiritual realities with Spirit-taught words" (1 Cor. 2:13, NIV). "But people who aren't spiritual can't receive these truths from God's Spirit. It all sounds foolish to them and they can't understand it, for only those who are spiritual can understand what the spirit means" (1 Cor. 2:14, NLT).

The aspect of mankind that is built up spiritually is the part that interacts with God and gets inspiration through His Word. Paul further added, "There is a natural body, and there is a spiritual body... Howbeit that *was* not first which is spiritual, but that which is natural; and afterward that which is spiritual" (1 Cor. 15:44, 46). It is not the natural body (our flesh) that is built up into a spiritual house, but our intellect (the faculty of reasoning and objective understanding). While we still maintain our natural body, we are required to also have the spiritual nature as well. With how many natures are we presented?

> And so it is written, The first man Adam was made a living soul... The first man *is* of the earth, earthy: the second man *is* the Lord from heaven. As *is* the earthy, such *are* they also that are earthy: and as *is* the heavenly, such *are* they also that are heavenly. And as we have borne the image of the earthy, we shall also bear the image of the heavenly. (1 Corinthians 15: 45, 47–49)

Here we are presented with two different natures from two different individuals: Adam and Jesus, with a natural body of the earth and a spiritual mind of the heavens, respectively. As we bear the image of the first, so shall we bear the image of the second. "Let this mind be in you, which was also in Christ Jesus" (Phil. 2:5).

> Through Christ, God works to bring man back to his first relation to his Creator and to correct the disorganizing influences brought in by Satan.... Christ came to our world, **clothing His divinity with humanity, that humanity might touch humanity and divinity grasp divinity.** Amid the din of selfishness He could say to men: Return to your center--God. He Himself made it possible for man to do this by carrying out in this world the principles of heaven. (White, *Testimonies for the Church*, vol. 6, p. 237)

Life and Death

In the beginning, God made humanity perfect, holy, and pure. They were endowed with noble powers, a well-balance mind, love, joy, peace, longsuffering, gentleness, kindness, faith, meekness, and self-control. These traits were perfectly endowed after the image and likeness of God. Adam and Eve were placed as God's representatives over the lower orders of being. Their countenances bore the ruddy tint of health and glowed with the light of life and joy. Their natures were in harmony with the will of God. "His affections were pure, His appetites and passions were under the control of reason.... He was lofty stature and perfect symmetry" (White 1890, p. 45). Both in outward resemblance and character, mankind bore the image of God.

> *Freedom exists when there are multiple options and also the right and power to make choices between those options*

God made humans as free moral agents who could be capable of making choices between two options. They were endowed with full rights to yield or withhold obedience with the absence of constraint. It is interesting to note that perfect freedom does not exist in an environment where there is only one way or option. Otherwise, it's not freedom at all. Freedom exists when there are multiple options and also the right and power to make choices between those options. The Bible says, "Now the Lord is that Spirit: and where the Spirit of the Lord *is*, there *is* liberty" (2 Cor. 3:17).

In God's presence, there is liberty, and all who abide before Him dwell in perfect freedom. Because freedom is part of His nature, and for mankind to perfectly reflect His image, He places before them two ways or options. God says, "I form the light, and create darkness: I make peace, and create evil: I the LORD do all these *things*" (Isa. 45:7).

Though humans were created innocent and holy, they were not placed beyond the possibility of making wrong choices. That is what is truly called freedom. God desires that mankind's service and loyalty to Him must be voluntary and not by force. They need to choose to serve God as the Creator. That was why God said, "See, I have set before thee this day life and good, and death and evil" (Deut. 30:15).

Though God did not create mankind with the knowledge of good and evil, He gave them an important rule: "Of every tree of the garden thou mayest freely eat: But of the tree of the knowledge of good and evil, thou shalt not eat of it: for in the day that thou eatest thereof thou shalt surely die" (Gen. 2:16, 17). Note that there were many good trees and one bad tree, and Adam and Eve had to make a vital choice. This choice was to prove and establish them before God. To maintain a balance, the two options were with no bias towards evil; otherwise, it would have been unfair.

For their decision capacity not to tilt to one side, God endowed them with high intellectual powers and allowed the two options to present their inducements before them so that their will could be put to the test. Thus, light and darkness, life and death, blessing and curse were placed before mankind to make a choice.

To woo humans towards the right path, God set before them a guide—the law of commandments which contain the benefits of allegiance. Obedience, perfect and perpetual, was the condition for eternal happiness. On this condition, mankind was to have access to the tree of life. "I call heaven and earth to record this day against you, *that* I have set before you life and death, blessing and cursing: therefore choose life, that both thou and thy seed may live" (Deut. 30:19).

God is omnipotent, omniscient, and immutable. He always pursues a straightforward course. His law is truth—immutable, eternal truth. His precepts are consistent with His attributes. Besides His inducement towards a right path, to allow equal play, humans "were also to be exposed to the temptations of Satan; but if they endured the trial, they would finally be placed beyond his power, to enjoy perpetual favor with God" (White 1890, p. 48).

If there were not multiple options to make choices, then people would not have been free moral agents, but mere automatons. Without freedom of choice, their obedience would not have been voluntary, but forced. There could have been no development of character. Such a course would have been contrary to God's divine plan in dealing with His creatures.

Adam and Eve

When Adam and Eve were placed in the Garden of Eden, they were on probation as free agents. The choice they were to make at that critical moment was to decide their destiny. Satan was permitted to manifest his inducements by way of temptation, and it was expected that they should overcome the enemy of humanity. Unfortunately, Adam and Eve made a wrong choice; they chose the way that seemed right to them. "And when the woman saw that the tree *was* good for food, and that it *was* pleasant to the eyes, and a tree to be desired to make *one* wise, she took of the fruit thereof, and did eat, and gave also unto her husband with her; and he did eat" (Gen. 3:6).

And by this, they chose the way of selfishness. They decided to live for themselves. The Bible says, "There is a way which seemeth right unto a man, but the end thereof *are* the ways of death." (Prov. 14:12). "Adam became a law to himself, and discord and unhappiness came into his life. A separation was made between him and God" (White 1990, p. 37).

The Image of Man

"And Adam lived an hundred and thirty years, and begat *a son* in his own likeness, after his image; and called his name Seth: And the days of Adam after he had begotten Seth were eight hundred years: and he begat sons and daughters" (Gen. 5:3, 4). Adam's descendants took after the fallen nature of their parents, with the possibility of yielding to temptation. "Therefore as by the offence of one *judgment came* upon all men to condemnation… For as by one man's disobedience many were made sinners" (Rom 5:18, 19). "For as in Adam all die…" (1 Cor. 15:22); "… and so death passed upon all men, for that all have sinned" (Rom. 15:12).

The children of Adam partook of his mortal nature, and by their sins, they died spiritually. In the light of justification and sanctification, no one can take a step towards the spiritual life unless Jesus draws and strengthens the soul and leads the person to experience repentance. The Scripture says, "And you *hath he quickened*, who were dead in trespasses and sins… Even when we were dead in sins, hath quickened us together with Christ, (by grace ye are saved;)" (Eph. 2:1, 5).

For people to live a spiritual life, they must first have an awakened spirit, aroused from a stupor, alive and not dead. However, can we live a spiritual life without knowing what constitutes mankind's spirit? No, of course not.

The Spirit of Man

From our study so far, we saw that there are a natural body and spiritual body—Adam from the earth and the Lord Jesus, the lifegiving source, from heaven. And just as we bear the image of the natural, so we are to bear the image of the spiritual. Having this in mind, our question is, how do we bear the image of this Lifegiving Lord of heaven?

"God *is* a Spirit" (John 4:24). If God is a spirit, this implies that we are also required to bear that same image. Now how do we partake of His image? The Bible says, "That which is born of the flesh is flesh; and that which is born of the Spirit is spirit" (John.3:6). In other words, the change or transformation we are talking about here can only occur through a rebirth. By being born of the Spirit, we become of the Spirit.

How does the rebirth take place? "The wind bloweth where it listeth, and thou hearest the sound thereof, but canst not tell whence it cometh, and whither it goeth: so is every one that is born of the Spirit." Therefore, we may not exactly decipher or perfectly describe how the rebirth takes place, but our inability to describe how the change occurred cannot nullify the reality of the rebirth. Describing it further, the Bible says, "For as many as are led by the Spirit of God, they are the sons of God" (Rom. 8:14).

It is by the new birth that we become sons and daughters of God. How do we know precisely when the change occurs? "The Spirit itself beareth witness with our spirit, that we are the children of God" (v. 16). "But *there is* a spirit in man: and the inspiration of the Almighty giveth them understanding" (Job 32:8).

It is by the inspiration of the Holy Spirit of God in us that we are confirmed as the children of God. Regarding our spirit, God's Word says, "The burden of the word of the LORD for Israel, saith the LORD, which stretcheth forth the heavens, and layeth the foundation of the earth, and formeth the spirit of man within him" (Zech. 12:1). Here we are told that the spirit of mankind was formed within by God. If that be the case, what is the likeness of mankind's spirit? What language did the Scripture employ to describe the spirit of mankind?

Some people think that a spirit is a ghost—some sort of bodyless phantom that floats around. Is that what God's Word says? Certainly not! According to *The American Heritage Dictionary*, "ghost" means "The spirit of a dead person, especially one believed to appear in bodily likeness to living persons or to haunt former habitats." The Bible calls this a familiar spirit.

The Lamp of God

"The spirit of man *is* the candle of the LORD, searching all the inward parts of the belly" (Prov. 20:27). The original Hebrew word *nerah* means "lamp or candle." *Nerah* is used to typify the spirit of mankind. Because God's Word likens mankind's spirit to a light-bearing vessel, that was why "lamp" was used in connection with the ten virgins. "Then shall the kingdom of heaven be likened unto ten virgins, who took their lamps, and went forth to meet the bridegroom" (Matt. 25:1).

In this parable, the wise and foolish virgins both had lamps, but the only difference is that the five wise virgins had extra oil in their vessels, while the foolish did not. Besides giving light within lamps, for what other purpose is oil used? "Then shalt thou take the anointing oil, and pour *it* upon his head, and anoint him" (Ex. 29:7). Olive oil was used in OT times for anointing, but in NT times we read, "How God anointed Jesus of Nazareth with the Holy Ghost and with power" (Acts 10:38).

The oil with which the virgins filled their lamps represents the Holy Spirit. In Zechariah 4, "the two olive trees empty the golden oil out of themselves through the golden pipes into the golden bowl from which the lamps of the sanctuary are fed. The golden oil represents the Holy Spirit" (White 1923, p. 188).

Having proven in God's Word that mankind's spirit is a light-bearing vessel, what description was further used in inspired writing? The lamp is identified as "an outward semblance of religion… a lamp of profession" (White 1955, p. 118). What is the flame, the fire itself, in the lamp? In God's Word, we are told, "*Is* not my word like as a fire? saith the LORD" (Jer. 23:29).

Of the Word of God, the psalmist wrote, "The entrance of Thy Word giveth light; it giveth understanding to the simple" (119:105). "It is as a light shining in a dark place. As we search its pages, light enters the heart, illuminating the mind. By this light we see what we ought to be" ("Our Guide-book," *The Signs of the Times*, June 26, 1901).

The oil (Holy Spirit), lamp (semblance of religion), and flame of fire (God's Word) combined make humans spiritual beings. It is that which is external that is represented by the lamp, but it is worthless without oil and fire. Jesus Christ is the Light Bearer to the world—to every individual soul; the Holy Spirit is the oil; Jesus does the trimming, and His blessed and precious Word illuminates the soul. It is only when the Holy Spirit vivifies the soul that the very hand that lit it then trims and sparks the flame. This thought is forcibly brought out in the parable of the ten virgins.

When the light of God shines in the soul, it is then said that one is spiritual. However, in sin one is in darkness. The wise man said, "For there shall be no reward to the evil *man*; the Lamp of the wicked shall be put out" (Prov. 24:20). That is to say that when any person turns away from God, his or her light goes off. This condition is called spiritual death. Jesus' appeal is "Take heed therefore that the light which is in thee be not darkness. If thy whole body therefore *be* full of light, having no part dark, the whole shall be full of light, as when the bright shining of a candle doth give thee light" (Luke 11:35, 36).

Now having correctly identified the spiritual components of mankind, our next important question is, where do the burning flames of the spirit in us sit? "Who hath also sealed us, and given the earnest of the Spirit in our hearts" (2 Cor. 1:22). The seat of the burning flame of mankind's spirit is right in the heart/mind. That was why the apostle Paul said, "And be renewed in the spirit of your mind" (Eph. 4:23). Therefore, the light of God's Spirit shines forth from our hearts and "Their light will shine clear and distinct amid the moral darkness, for it is the light of the gospel, which 'is the power of God unto salvation'" ("Christ the Power that Draws Men to God," *The Signs of the Times*, November 16, 1891).

Body, Spirit, and Soul

"And the very God of peace sanctify you wholly; and *I pray God* your whole spirit and soul and body be preserved blameless unto the coming of our Lord Jesus Christ" (1 Thess. 5:23). The Bible here seems to present three dimensions to every person: body, spirit, and soul. Does this passage negate the biblical teaching that mankind does not have an immortal soul?

Before we discuss what this passage tells us, let's focus a little on the basics. The Bible says, "And the LORD God formed man *of* the dust of the ground, and breathed into his nostrils the breath of life; and man became a living soul" (Gen. 2:7). While it is true that humans were originally made living souls by God, the living soul was not put into them, but the breath of life which was put into the molded dust from the ground made them living souls. The word "soul," Hebrew *nephesh*, and Greek *psyche* have diverse meanings that could apply to "soul," "life," "person," "heart," "mind," "creature/beast," "body," "death," "humanity," or "ghost."

The word translated "breath" in Hebrew is *ruach* (Greek *pneuma*), and it has the same multiple meanings that *nephesh* and *psyche* do for "soul." Each Bible text is better understood by its context. With this understanding, we are ready to review the meaning of 1 Thessalonians 5:23.

In dividing a person into three aspects or components, Paul was not addressing the mortal or immortal aspects of a person; instead he was addressing the entire spiritual component, in which he described the soul as the mind, the body as the flesh, and the spirit as the feeling or emotion. How does the emotion or feeling in this context represent our spirit?

The Emotional Effect

"As for me, *is* my complaint to man? and if *it were so*, why should not my spirit be troubled" (Job. 21:4)? In other words, the spirit is the part of a person that can be troubled. "I remembered God, and was troubled: I complained, and my spirit was overwhelmed" (Ps. 77:3). The spirit is the part of a person that can be overwhelmed or experience a strong emotional effect. "I Daniel was grieved in my spirit in the midst of *my* body, and the visions of my head troubled me" (Dan. 7:15). Here we see that a spirit is the part of the body that can be grieved.

In Mark's gospel we read, "And immediately when Jesus perceived in his spirit that they so reasoned within themselves, he said unto them, why reason ye these things in your hearts" (2:8)? A spirit is the part of a person that can perceive or understand things (intuition). John wrote, "When Jesus therefore saw her weeping, and the Jews also weeping which came with her, he groaned in the spirit, and was troubled" (John 11:33). The spirit is the part of a person that can groan.

From our study so far, we saw that God's Word kindles the burning flame of our spiritual life and plants in our hearts the nine principles of God's character: love, joy, peace, longsuffering, gentleness, goodness, faith, meekness, and temperance. These are not just mere mental principles; they are strong emotional attachments that enable us to feel for others and care for them. For example:

> [Faith and feeling] are distinct as the east is from the west.... When our faith grasps the blessing, then the blessing is ours, for our faith has got hold of it, and when our faith brings the blessing down to us--when the dark clouds scatter and divine rays of light from Jesus illumine our darkness--then it is no more faith, it is feeling. The evidence has come and it is feeling that has swallowed up the faith. This view of faith and feeling seemed to enlighten some minds and we had a most powerful conference meeting. (White, *Manuscript Releases*, vol. 5, pp. 206, 207)

The Two-sided Brain

The human brain is an intricate organ. At approximately 3 pounds, it contains about 100 billion neurons and 100 trillion connections. Your brain is command central of all you think, feel, and do.

Your brain is divided into two halves, or hemispheres. Within each half, particular regions control certain functions.

The two sides of your brain look very much alike, but there's a huge difference in how they process information. (healthline, http://1ref.us/qr, [accessed 11/15/2018])

According to Psychobiologist and Nobel Prize winner Roger W. Sperry, our brain is divided into two sides. His study came to light in the 1960s, and the subject was medically reviewed by Deborah Weatherspoon, Ph.D., RN, CRNA, COI on January 18, 2017.

According to Sperry's dated research, the left brain is also connected to:
- logic
- sequencing
- linear thinking
- mathematics
- facts
- thinking in words (Ibid.)

One can say the left side of the brain is the center of reasoning, memory, and will powers. This is the side where information is compartmentalized, sieved, and sifted. This is the center of our thought and reasoning. The memory is like the central database where all incoming information is stored. The reasoning power is the analyzing, critical, and logical side of the brain. The will is the deciding power in mankind.

The right brain is more visual and intuitive. It's sometimes referred to as the analog brain. It has a more creative and less organized way of thinking.

Sperry's dated research suggests the right brain is also connected to:
- imagination
- holistic thinking
- intuition
- arts
- rhythm
- nonverbal cues
- feeling visualization
- daydreaming (Ibid.)

On this, we can say the right brain is the center of the conscience, intuition, emotions, affections, feelings, and imagination. Based on this understanding, what constitutes the whole human mind are the combined powers of these two sides of the brain. "Each faculty of the mind and each muscle has its distinctive office, and all require to be exercised in order to become properly developed and retain healthful vigor" (White 1898, p. 69).

The left and right sides of the brain are in a nutshell identified as the thought and feeling (soul and spirit) centers, respectively. Feelings and emotions are subject to the reasoning powers of the human mind. One's conscience is an endowed ability to discern right and wrong, while the intuition is the ability to discern secret things, as well as sense the Lord and His presence. From the account in Mark 2:8, we saw that Jesus perceived or understood in His spirit what they were thinking.

"The brain nerves which communicate with the entire system are the only medium through which Heaven can communicate with man, and affect his inmost life. Whatever disturbs the circulation of the electric currents in the nervous system, lessens the strength of the vital powers, and the result is a deadening of the sensibilities of the mind" (White 1898, pp. 193, 194).

Avenues of the Mind

Naturally, God designed that we should be using our whole brain when doing things.

> The brain is the capital of the body, the seat of all the nervous forces and of mental action. The nerves proceeding from the brain control the body. By the brain nerves, mental impressions are conveyed to all the nerves of the body as by telegraph wires; and they control the vital action of every part of the system. All the organs of motion are governed by the communications they receive from the brain. (White, *Healthful Living*, p. 193)

It will also interest you to know that the mind receives information via five avenues or senses: sound, sight, smell, taste, and touch. Everything that people have learned about the world around them has funneled through these senses. They are not necessarily perfect; they may be damaged by accident; they may become impaired through age and unable to distinguish good from bad. The five senses, therefore, are not the most reliable means of information.

God knows this, and that's why He gave His Word and the Holy Spirit, a sure foundation and accurate source of information. Often the information we get through our five senses contradicts what we read in God's Word and the ministration of the Holy Spirit within our spirit. There is a battle between the Word and the backlog of information that we have gained throughout our earthly life.

"It is our privilege, as children of God, to hold fast the profession of our faith without wavering. At times the masterly power of temptation seems to tax our willpower to the uttermost and to exercise faith seems utterly contrary to all the evidences of sense or emotion; but our will must be kept on God's side" (White 1977, p. 687).

The Areas of Temptation

Satan operates in the sensual realm, through what we see, hear, touch or feel, smell, and taste. This was the approach he used on the first humans. They saw the fruit was good and pleasing to the eyes, so they plucked (touched) and ate (taste) (see Gen. 3:6). The five senses are avenues of temptation the enemy uses to tempt the flesh with an appealing hook. We are weak in these areas and he knows it. By laying twisted paths of temptation before us, he leads us into a deeper, lost condition, further away from the truth of spiritual life.

Living in the realm of the five senses, the devil dominated us through lust, illicit desires, and unclean practices that lead a person to demonic influence. He has no feeling of warmth.

He attacks the flesh through the senses, with our desires and the imagination of sinful lust of the flesh and eyes. He burns evil passion into our souls. He allures us with the love of money and material possessions and entangles us with wealth and power.

> *In the world today, there is a tremendous battle for the mind and spirit of mankind. Political parties, advertisements, and the media, in general, are all clamoring for our attention*

> Satanic agencies took possession of men. The bodies of human beings, made for the dwelling place of God, became the habitation of demons. The senses, the nerves, the organs of men were worked by supernatural agencies in the indulgence of the vilest lust. The very stamp of demons was impressed upon the countenances of men. Human faces reflected the expression of the legions of evil with which men were possessed. (White, *The Ministry of Healing*, p. 142)

Therefore, the spirit and mind are the places of great importance in the daily life of a believing Christian. It is significant because it is the key to power, and the Word of God emphasizes it. In the world today, there is a tremendous battle for the mind and spirit of mankind. Political parties, advertisements, and the media, in general, are all clamoring for our attention.

The Spirit of Prophecy reveals that it's the purity of the mind and spirit that constitutes our moral character. The servant of the Lord said, "If the thoughts are wrong the feelings will be wrong, and the thoughts and feelings combined make up the moral character. When you decide that as Christians you are not required to restrain your thoughts and feelings you are brought under the influence of evil angels and invite their presence and their control" (White 1889, p. 310).

Whenever we are alive in the Spirit, we will also have a living conscience. Our feelings and emotions become sanctified and bear good fruit. However, if we are dead in the Spirit, our conscience equally becomes dead, and our emotions and feelings manifest the opposite of the nine fruits of the Holy Spirit.

Life in the Spirit

In the beginning, mankind was designed with dual life—the natural life sustained by simple oxygen and a spiritual life by the Holy Spirit. That is why, when God breathed into mankind the breath of life (see Gen 2:7), that breath was both oxygen and the Holy Spirit. "All the while my breath *is* in me, and the spirit of God *is* in my nostrils" (Job 27:3).

The Holy Spirit is the life spark and upholder of the breath of life in mankind's nostrils. This is what Job was saying. The Holy Spirit is also the sustainer of mankind's spiritual life. The beloved apostle John says, "It is the Spirit that gives life; the flesh profits nothing" (John 6:63, NIV).

"As our natural life is sustained by physical food, so our spiritual life is to be sustained by spiritual food, even the words of Christ. The Gospel, believed and lived, means eternal life. It gives spiritual health and vigor. It enables us to show in the daily life the fruits of the Spirit" ("The Bread of Life," *The Signs of the Times*, October 3, 1900).

Unfortunately, after Adam and Eve fell, they lost their spiritual lives and the active burning flame of God's Spirit in their souls and were left with a natural, fleshly life that profits nothing. Notwithstanding, glory be to God the Father, who through the death of His Son Jesus Christ on the cross of Calvary has restored humanity's spiritual life to all who truly accept Him as their personal Lord and Savior. The Bible says, "to them gave he power to become the sons of God, *even* to them that believe on his name" (John 1:12).

Jesus' death and resurrection have given mankind the privilege and opportunity of once again experiencing a spiritual life. "The Author of this spiritual life is unseen, and the exact method by which that life is imparted and sustained, it is beyond the power of human philosophy to explain. Yet the operations of the Spirit are always in harmony with the written word. As in the natural, so in the spiritual world" (White 1911, p. 284).

Please note that there are two lives in the picture: natural and spiritual. "For to be carnally minded *is* death; but to be spiritually minded *is* life and peace" (Rom. 8:6). Whenever we give our lives to Christ, the natural life is subdued by divine power. Inspiration reveals that:

> The natural life is preserved moment by moment by divine power; yet it is not sustained by a direct miracle, but through the use of blessings placed within our reach. So the spiritual life is sustained by the use of those means that Providence has supplied. If the follower of Christ would grow up "unto a perfect man, unto the measure of the stature of the fullness of Christ" (Ephesians 4:13), he must eat of the bread of life and drink of the water of salvation. (White, *The Acts of the Apostles*, pp. 284, 285)

New Birth Experience

"That which is born of the flesh is flesh; and that which is born of the Spirit is spirit" (John 3:6). Through the new birth experience, the flesh is cleansed of its sin. "For if you are living according to the flesh, you must die; but if by the Spirit you are putting to death the deeds of the body, you will live" (Rom. 8:13, NIV).

From the pen of inspiration, we are told, "The Holy Spirit is the breath of spiritual life in the soul. The impartation of the Spirit is the impartation of the life of Christ. It imbues the receiver with the attributes of Christ" (White 1898, p. 805).

God wants us to live a spiritual life today. Rebirth is the channel by which the spiritual life can flow in us and give life to our bodies. This is His ultimate goal for every believer. "Nicodemus saith unto him, How can a man be born when he is old? can he enter the second time into his mother's womb, and be born? Jesus answered, Verily, verily, I say unto thee, Except a man be born of water and *of* the Spirit, he cannot enter into the kingdom of God" (John 3:5–8).

What is the meaning of being born of water? "That he might sanctify and cleanse it with the washing of water by the word" (Eph. 5:26). "Being born again, not of corruptible seed, but of incorruptible, by the word of God, which liveth and abideth for ever" (1 Peter 1:23).

To be born of water, in a primary sense, means to be cleansed and sanctified by His Word, while in a secondary sense, it points to a public testimony of a union with Christ. What is the meaning of being born of the Spirit? "But if the Spirit of Him who raised Jesus from the dead dwells in you, Him who raised up Christ Jesus from the dead will also give life to your mortal bodies through His Spirit who dwell in you… For as many as are led by the Spirit of God, they are the sons of God" (Rom. 8:11, 14).

The two lives in the picture are the flesh and the Spirit. To be born of water and the Spirit describes the two life experiences. The Bible says, "Therefore we are buried with him by baptism into death: that like as Christ was raised up from the dead by the glory of the Father, even so we also should walk in newness of life" (6:4).

Water baptism, which includes purification through God's Word and a public attestation through descending into the water, symbolically represents the cleansing of the flesh so it can live a new life in Christ. The baptism of the Holy Spirit is the resurrection of our spiritual lives, and "If we live in the Spirit," God wants "us [to] also walk in the Spirit" (Gal. 5:25).

Although the first is the primary work of the Holy Spirit, the second is the perfecting work of the Holy Spirit. Many of us today are living our lives in the flesh, devoid of the spiritual touch. God's original plan is that the baptism of the Holy Spirit is to immediately follow after we had our water baptism.

However, many have lost sight of the fact that water baptism is a symbol of the death and resurrection of Christ. We are charged to be dead to sin before we are buried with Christ publicly in a watery grave so that we can rise to a newness of life in Him through the baptism of the Holy Spirit. Many have not made the right spiritual progress in their lives. From the pen of inspiration, we are told, "The new birth is a rare experience in this age of the world. This is the reason why there are so many perplexities in the churches. Many, so many, who assume the name of Christ, are unsanctified and unholy. They have been baptized, but they were buried alive. Self did not die, and therefore they did not rise to newness of life in Christ" (White 1956, p. 1075).

"Whosoever is born of God doth not commit sin; for his seed remaineth in him: and he cannot sin, because he is born of God" (1 John 3:9). This is God's great objective. Therefore, brethren, to achieve this goal, He gave His only begotten Son so that whoever believes in Him should not perish, but have everlasting life. "That if you confess with your mouth Jesus as

Lord, and believe in your heart that God raised him from the dead, you will be saved" (Rom. 10:9).

The moment a sinner accepts Christ by faith, that moment he or she is pardoned. The righteousness of Christ is imputed to that person. "The grace of Christ in the heart will always promote spiritual life, and spiritual advancement will be made" (White 1973, p. 324).

> The Spirit of God, with its vivifying power, must be in every human agent, that every spiritual muscle and sinew may be in exercise. Without the Holy Spirit, without the breath of God, there is torpidity of conscience, loss of spiritual life. Many who are without spiritual life have their names on the church records, but they are not written in the Lamb's book of life. They may be joined to the church, but they are not united to the Lord. They may be diligent in the performance of a certain set of duties, and may be regarded as living men; but many are among those who have "a name that thou livest, and art dead." (White, *The SDA Bible Commentary*, vol. 4, p. 1166)

First World War

It was said that during World War I, an American pilot took off from an airfield located in Arabia. Little did he know that while the plane was on the ground, a large rat crawled up inside the plane's cockpit. While in the air, the pilot became suspicious of the rat's presence when he heard some gnawing behind him. He immediately realized that the sound he was hearing was the sound of a rat.

Alarmed at what could turn into a disastrous situation, the pilot remembered that rats could not live at high altitudes, so he simply pointed his airplane up and climbed to altitudes where breathing was difficult. After some time at the high altitude, the gnawing stopped. When he landed on the ground, he found that the gnawing rat died.

This is what happens in one's spiritual life. The gnawing rat could represent our spiritual struggles; it could represent the darkness of the evil one pressing upon our souls to shut out Jesus from our view; it could represent one challenge or the other in our lives. The Lord allows this to befall us because we are still living at the lower altitudes of the spiritual life. He wants us to ascend higher. In the Holy Scriptures, we are told, "And it shall come to pass in that day, *that* his burden shall be taken away from off thy shoulder, and his yoke from off thy neck and the yoke shall be destroyed because of the anointing" (Isa. 10:27).

Here we are told that the anointing will break the yoke. What does the original Hebrew say? To mix Hebrew and English verbiage, the text reads, "The yoke shall be destroyed because of *shamen*." What does the word *shamen* mean? It means "oil," although the King James Version translators understood it to be the equivalent of "anointing." However, there is nowhere in the Hebrew Bible where the word *shamen* ("oil") by itself means "anointing."

What, then, is the text saying? It means "fatness," which would produce a literal translation of "the yoke will be destroyed because of the fat." What does *that* mean? The New International Version expresses it well: "in that day their burden will be lifted from your shoulders, their yoke from your neck; the yoke will be broken because you have grown so fat."

Do you get the picture? Here is an ox with a yoke on its neck, enslaving it to the will of its master and forcing it to a life of servitude, but eventually, it gets so healthy and fat that the yoke bursts from its neck. That ox is now free! And that is a picture for each of us when we find ourselves bound, oppressed, or beaten into submission by the enemy. We feed our spirits with the living Word day and night, continue in worship, praise, prayer, and communion, and little by little; we get so healthy and strong—so "fat"—that suddenly the yoke of oppression must burst. The fatness destroys the yoke. Now you know what the word really says.

What's Our Greatest Need today? A revival of true godliness among us is the greatest and most urgent of all our needs. To seek this should be our first work...A revival needs be expected only in answer to prayer. (White, Selected Messages, Book 1.p. 121)

I tell you that there must be a thorough revival among us. There must be a converted ministry. There must be confessions, repentance, and conversions. Many who are preaching the Word need the transforming grace of Christ in their hearts. They should let nothing stand in the way of their making thorough work before it shall be forever too late. (White, Last Day Events, p. 189.2)

A revival and a reformation must take place, under the ministration of the Holy Spirit. Revival and reformation are two different things. Revival signifies a renewal of spiritual life, a quickening of the powers of mind and heart, a resurrection from spiritual death. Reformation signifies a reorganization, a change in ideas and theories, habits and practices. Reformation will not bring forth the good fruit of righteousness unless it is connected with the revival of the Spirit. Revival and reformation are to do their appointed work, and in doing this work they must blend.(White, The Review and Herald,Feb. 25, 1902)

CHAPTER 4

BATTLE OF THE DARK REALM

One of the things that we all must know is that life is controlled by things happening in the spirit realm. Indeed, we are living in a very crucial time in human history. When we talk about personal success, national development, scientific advancements, marital bliss, or anything else in life, these are all physical expressions of the things that are going on unseen. They are inspired either by God or the devil.

What we see in the physical realm are the final products of all kinds of equations and arrangements that have been concluded in the spirit realm. Please don't misunderstand me; God still remains the final arbiter, because He is the one who created both the visible and invisible things. "For by him were all things created, that are in heaven, and that are in earth, visible and invisible, whether *they be* thrones, or dominions, or principalities, or powers: all things were created by him, and for him" (Col. 1:16).

Thus, the invisible things were created by God, both in heaven and on earth. As we have already proven, God is Spirit, but besides Him, who else is a spirit? "And of the angels he saith, Who maketh his angels spirits, and his ministers a flame of fire" (Heb 1:7). God's angels are spirits, while His earthly children are made flaming fire through His Word.

Besides God and His angels, who else is a spirit? "For he had commanded the unclean spirit to come out of the man. For oftentimes it had caught him: and he was kept bound with chains and in fetters; and he brake the bands, and was driven of the devil into the wilderness" (Luke 8:29). Here we see that besides God and His angels, the devil and his angels are also identified as spirits. Speaking about their involvement in the earthly activities, the Bible says, "We know that we are children of God and that the whole world is under the control of the evil one" (1 John 5:19, NIV).

The world is immersed in darkness, and we as believers must know how to navigate through it to live effective Christian lives. Realizing how intense the wicked activities of the enemy of human soul would be in the last days, John the revelator, in a holy vision, saw an angel crying, "Woe to the inhabiters of the earth and of the sea! For the devil is come down unto you, having great wrath, because he knoweth that he hath but a short time" (Rev. 12:12). The angel is saying that there will be trouble upon mankind as a result of satanic activities in these last days.

Demonic Possession

The idea that people can be possessed by evil spirits against their will is as old as mankind. Although medical science remains skeptical, some psychiatrists believe demonic possession is indeed very real. The Bible says, **"And the people with one accord gave heed unto those things which Philip spake, hearing and seeing the miracles which he did. For unclean spirits, crying with loud voice, came out of many that were possessed *with them*: and many taken with palsies, and that were lame, were healed"** (Acts 8:6, 7). Also, **"And at even, when the sun did set, they brought unto him all that were diseased, and them that were possessed with devils"** (Mark 1:32).

> *The world is immersed in darkness, and we as believers must know how to navigate through it to live effective Christian lives*

To force an uninvited spirit to vacate a possessed person is extremely difficult. As you can see, Jesus spoke with a voice of authority and set the captive free. The demonic spirit made a last effort to rend the life from his victim before he was forced to depart. Then the man who had been possessed stood before the wondering people happy in the freedom of self-possession. **"Then went the devils out of the man, and entered into the swine: and the herd ran violently down a steep place into the lake, and were choked. When they that fed *them* saw what was done, they fled, and went and told *it* in the city and in the country"** (Luke 8:33, 34).

"In nearly every instance, Christ addressed the demon as an intelligent entity, commanding him to come out of his victim and to torment him no more. The worshipers at Capernaum, beholding his mighty power, **"were all amazed, and spake among themselves, saying, What a word is this! for with authority and power he commandeth the unclean spirits, and they come out"** (White 1888 p. 515).

Can a child have a demon? Yes, children can have demons just like adults do. The phenomenon can be traced through history and around the world. **"And one of the multitude answered and said, Master, I have brought unto thee my son, which hath a dumb spirit… And he asked his father, How long is it ago since this came unto him? And he said, Of a child"** (Mark 9:17, 21).

The term "young child" can mean an "infant" (Greek *paidion*). *Paidion* is used for John the Baptist when he was eight days old (see Luke 1:59, 66, 76, 80). It is used for Jesus when he was born (see 2:17), eight days old (see v. 21), and forty days old (see vs. 27, 40). In fact, *paidion* is used for Jesus when the shepherds were there on the night of His birth. Perhaps the child may have very well been born with an evil spirit. Literally translated, the father was saying that his son was possessed from infancy.

A demon-possessed person can be in a condition of great suffering, much like the daughter of the Syro-Phenician woman was grievously vexed with a devil (see Mark 7:26–30), one **"possessed with a devil, blind, and dumb"** (Matt. 12:22), the youth who had a dumb spirit that often **"cast him into the fire, and into the waters, to destroy him"** (Mark 9:17–27), and the maniac who was tormented by **"a spirit of an unclean devil"** (Luke 4:33-36).

> Those possessed with devils are usually represented as being in a condition of great suffering; yet there were exceptions to this rule. For the sake of obtaining supernatural power, some welcomed the satanic influence. These of course had no conflict with the demons. Of this class were those who possessed the spirit of divination—Simon Magus, Elymas the sorcerer, and the damsel who followed Paul and Silas at Philippi. (White, *The Great Controversy*, p. 516)

How do we overcome this ruthless and malicious enemy?

Intelligence

During the Vietnam War, America suffered severely in the hands of Vietnam. The resilient Vietnamese shocked the world, but historians and military experts later discovered why the mighty US was nearly subdued. Until they discovered that North Vietnam was landmine-infested, American soldiers perished in droves throughout their engagement between 1964 and 1975, when they finally pulled out all the remaining soldiers from the Vietnamese territory.

Why then was this war disgraceful for America? The reason is that the soldiers were zealous to go into battle for their country, but they did not have the requisite knowledge about that warzone. It was a lack of adequate intelligence. They paid dearly for that error. Zeal without adequate knowledge is very dangerous. Most Christians are very uncomfortable thinking and talking about Satan.

Secular military leaders know from experience that the more you know about your enemy's warzone, purposes, tactics, strengths, and weaknesses, the greater advantage you have on the battlefield. When you go out to do battle, it is important to know something about the enemy you face. In fact, knowing your enemy is so reasonable and logical that military leaders call this information intelligence.

It is sensible for us to spend a little time learning about the enemy of souls and how he attacks God's children so we can be on our guard every moment. It is because many have chosen to be ignorant of the enemy that families and churches today are under a serious siege.

> The children of God are not to expect an easy time in this life. There are battles to be fought. "We wrestle not against flesh and blood, but against principalities, against powers, against the rulers of the darkness of this world, against spiritual wickedness in high places." We are not left alone to engage in this conflict. Jesus is the captain of our salvation. He clothed His divinity with humanity, and took the field himself, that He might teach us how to fight the battles of the Lord. He says, "Lo, I come: in the volume of the book it is written of me, I delight to do thy will, O my God: yea, thy law is within my heart." ("A Teacher Sent from God," *The Review and Herald*, April 30, 1901)

Dear brothers and sisters, in every soul, two powers are struggling earnestly for victory. Hour by hour, in the sight of the heavenly universe, the conflict goes forward. A spiritual battle rages in the lives of believers, a conflict not merely with flesh and blood, but with despotisms, empires, and forces that control and govern this dark world with their spiritual hosts of evil, now arraying themselves against every believer in the heavenly places.

Spiritual Warfare

The apostle Paul made the following inspiring statement: "For we are not wrestling with flesh and blood [contending only with physical opponents], but against the despotisms, against the powers, against [the master spirits who are] the world rulers of this present darkness, against the spirit forces of wickedness in heavenly [supernatural] sphere" (Eph. 6:12, AMP).

This is true. We are indeed not wrestling with flesh and blood. The opposition to mankind that we meet daily is nothing but a satanic front.

There is someone behind this opposition. It is the prince of the powers of darkness with his evil angels.

The word "despot" means "a ruler who exercises absolute power, especially in a cruel and oppressive way." This description perfectly fits the evil one. It is interesting to note that ever since his fall, Satan has been leading out a rebellion; and he has been leading men and women astray. The warfare between good and evil has been progressively carried on for ages.

However, the tragedy of this crisis is that God's people are spiritually sleeping. We do not understand the devil's battleplan, and we are not spiritually ready for his last great attack. In a revelation, the servant of the Lord saw a more terrible power than that of Russia and all her red satellites invading God's people. She said, "I saw evil angels contending for souls, and angels of God resisting them. The conflict was severe. Evil angels were crowding about them, corrupting the atmosphere with their poisonous influence, and stupefying their sensibilities" (White 1930, p. 52).

"It is Satan's work to dethrone God from the heart, and to mold human nature into his own image of deformity. He stirs up all evil propensities, awakening unholy passions, thoughts and ambitions. His great desire is to degrade the human faculties, and brings man into captivity to sin" (Ibid., p. 54).

These spiritual hosts of evil have arrayed themselves against us in this cosmic warfare. Inspiration reveals that "The followers of Christ know little of the plots which Satan and his hosts are forming against them" (White 1930, p. 61). "His rage increases; we do not realize his power" (White 1958, p. 317). "While men are ignorant of his devices, this vigilant foe is upon their track every moment" (White 1911, p. 508).

Furthermore, we are told how Satan "directs his angels to lay their snares especially for those who are looking for the second coming of Christ and endeavoring to keep all the commandments of God" (White 1923, p, 472). Friends, we are living in a time when every true Christian must maintain a living connection with Christ. The world is flooded with sophistries of the enemy, and we are safe only as long as our lives are hidden in Jesus.

The Rulers of Darkness

The word "occult" comes from the Latin *occultus*, which means "hidden or secret power." Occultism is the belief in the existence of secret, mysterious, supernatural powers and the ability to bring them into the human sphere for manipulative purposes. An occultist is a person who uses these powers.

In God's Word, we are warned not to have anything to do with "the rulers of the darkness of this world" (Eph. 6:12).

"For if God spared not the angels that sinned, but cast *them* down to hell, and delivered *them* into chains of darkness, to be reserved unto judgment" (2 Peter 2:4). "And the angels which kept not their first estate, but left their own habitation, he hath reserved in everlasting chains under darkness unto the judgment of the great day" (Jude 6). Here the Word of God says that Satan was delivered into chains (or the realm of darkness) as a place of reservation (or abode) until the day of judgment.

"This then is the message which we have heard of him, and declare unto you, that God is light, and in him is no darkness at all" (1 John 1:5). "Before I go *whence* I shall not return, *even* to the land of darkness and the shadow of death; A land of darkness, as darkness *itself; and* of the shadow of death, without any order, and *where* the light *is* as darkness" (Job 10:21, 22). From these passages, we can deduce that God is light, and those who abide in His presence and do His will dwell in light. However, outside the presence of God is darkness.

Job additionally said that death is darkness; the dead are in darkness; those under the shadow of death are in darkness, and to be under the shadow of death is to be on death row, or under the condemnation of death. The phrase "kept in chain of darkness till the day of judgment," in a primary sense, points to the retributive judgment awaiting the devil and all his evil angels. It also points to the metaphysical realm where demons enshroud themselves in darkness.

The Work of Darkness

Today in our world, there are many secret societies officially operating and propagating satanism around the world. In various satanic activities, the use of rituals, spells, magical objects, incantations, spider web spells, projections, invocations, thought manipulations, and curses are very crucial. "Wherein in time past ye walked according to the course of this world, according to the prince of the power of the air, the spirit that now worketh in the children of disobedience" (Eph. 2.2).

There is a power that works in the air—satanic and wicked spirits in high places, working evil and mischief in our very atmosphere. Their operation is close to the very air we breathe and reaches realms beyond. In fact, in this realm, all kinds of spiritual filth are propagated for mankind's total destruction. However, God's promise is, "Behold, I give unto you power to tread on serpents and scorpions, and over all the power of the enemy: and nothing shall by any means hurt you" (Luke 10:19).

Fallen man is Satan's lawful captive. The mission of Christ was to rescue him from the power of his great adversary. Man is naturally inclined to follow Satan's suggestions, and he cannot successfully resist so terrible a foe unless Christ, the mighty Conqueror, dwells in him, guiding his desires, and giving him strength. God alone can limit the power of Satan.... Satan knows better than God's people the power that they can have over him when their strength is in Christ. When they humbly entreat the mighty Conqueror for help, the weakest believer in the truth, relying firmly upon Christ, can successfully repulse Satan and all his host....

Satan will [always try to] call to his aid legions of his angels to oppose the advance of even one soul, and, if possible, wrest it from the hand of Christ.... But if the one in danger perseveres, and in his helplessness casts himself upon the merits of the blood of Christ, our Saviour listens to the earnest prayer of faith, and sends a reinforcement of those angels that excel in strength to deliver him. Satan cannot endure to have his powerful rival appealed to, for he fears and trembles before His strength and majesty. At the sound of fervent prayer, Satan's whole host trembles. (White, *Our Father Cares*, pp. 215, 216)

Nothing but Christ's loving compassion, divine grace, and almighty power can enable us to battle the relentless foe and subdue the opposition of our hearts. What is our strength? The joy of the Lord is our strength. Let the love of Christ fill our hearts; then we shall be prepared to receive the power that He has for us.

The High Places

"And there they burnt incense in all the high places, as *did* the heathen whom the LORD carried away before them; and wrought wicked things to provoke the LORD to anger... Howbeit every nation made gods of their own, and put *them* in the houses of the high places which the Samaritans had made, every nation in their cities wherein they dwelt" (2 Kings 17:11, 29).

In the Scriptures, the phrase "high places" refers to shrines and altars dedicated to idols or any strange gods. In our modern times, these altars also include our modernized forms of satanic worship, those found in witchcraft covens, occult shrines, and those located in some of our homes and churches. Please note that satanic altars also include satanic rings, bangles, objects or materials of various kinds, that men used in making spiritual commands and worship. These are objects through which they offer sacrifices to the devil for evil purposes, sending their requests, and other spiritual wickedness against many ignorant men and women.

In these places of worship, satanic followers summon a demon or demons to perform a given action. Incantations are frequently in poetic form; they are multitudinous and have been passed down from generation to generation. They are usually spoken aloud by a witch into astral motion, where demons carry it into action.

Placing a spell, hex, or curse on someone refers to the act of calling up a demon and sending it to somebody to perform particular influences or damages. A curse is an occult process, phrase, sentence, or spoken words calling for injury by commanding evil spirits, operating in astral motion, to manipulate and fulfill certain incantations against a person or group of persons. The efficacy of every curse depends on the reason behind it, as well as the intensity of the mental or emotional focus that propelled it into psychic layers. When the intensity of any curse has reached such subtle layers, the evil spirits receive it for necessary manipulations.

And this is the war of wars because it is the war behind all wars. In it, the Christians appear to be in a decided minority. Arrayed against them are the rulers of the darkness of this world, the wicked spirits in high places—unseen but real, terrible, and ruthless. However, we have nothing to fear; God's Word has assured us that "As the bird by wandering, as the swallow by flying, so the curse causeless shall not come" (Prov. 26:2).

> Now, while our great High Priest is making the atonement for us, we should seek to become perfect in Christ. Not even by a thought could our Saviour be brought to yield to the power of temptation. Satan finds in human hearts some point where he can gain a foothold; some sinful desire is cherished, by means of which his temptations assert their power. But Christ declared of Himself: "The prince of this world cometh, and hath nothing in Me." John 14:30. Satan could find nothing in the Son of God that would enable him to gain the victory. He had kept His Father's commandments, and there was no sin in Him that Satan could use to his advantage. This is the condition in which those must be found who shall stand in the time of trouble. (White, *The Great* Controversy, p. 623)

Legal Permission

There are spiritual laws God has set that are in operation in our world. Even the demons abide by it. The Bible says, "Behold, I stand at the door, and knock: if any man hear my voice, and open the door, I will come in to him, and will sup with him, and he with me" (Rev. 3:20).

God will always seek our consent before He can come into our lives, and that's why the Scripture says He is standing at our door knocking. We are the ones who will decide whether or not Jesus will come into our lives. The reason is that He has given every one of us a free will and will never violate it.

It's a similar dynamic with demons. Though they want to use force, demons cannot oppress us unless we open the door to them. Our consent is their legal permission. There is only one way we give Satan our consent, and that way is sin. That's why the Bible says, "He that committeth sin is of the devil; for the devil sinneth from the beginning" (1 John 3:8).

Sin is an evil doorway, an avenue whereby Satan passes through to gain access into our lives. The Bible says, "Hast not thou made an hedge about him, and about his house, and about all that he hath on every side? thou hast blessed the work of his hands, and his substance is increased in the land" (Job 1:10).

All through Scripture, there is a hedge around every soul. This was done so that the enemy would not violate one's free will. What actions open our doorway to Satan? "He that diggeth a pit shall fall into it; and whoso breaketh an hedge, a serpent shall bite him" (Eccles. 10:8). Sin punctures a hole in the protective hedge around us; it opens the door and allows evil angels to attack us. The Scriptures are very plain. Any dealing with wicked agents opens a doorway in a person's life, thus attracting satanic power and infestation. The Bible says, "Regard not them that have familiar spirits, neither seek after wizards, to be defiled by them: I *am* the LORD your God" (Lev. 19:31).

Every person needs to be aware of the doorway in one's own life. It is also important to understand these doorways to be able to effectively share the gospel with others. For instance, any involvement with any kind of occult objects, role-playing games, and other materials, no matter how light or brief such may be, can open a door for evil infestation. Just one visit to a séance out of curiosity is enough to affect the rest of one's life.

The use of pornography also opens satanic doorways in our lives, allowing evil angels to easily gain access into our lives. Any participation in sexual perversions directly or indirectly opens up a person to the inflow of demons.

Abortion is another abomination which may result in demon infestation. This is because abortion is human sacrifice to the god of self, which is Satan. It is no different than the practice in Old Testament times of "passing children through fire," which was human sacrifice to the devil.

Rock n' roll, reggae, and other worldly music are also satanic doors. Rock records, crucifixes, rosaries, etc. are familiar objects. These must be removed from the house as they provide legal ground for the demons to come into our houses. "Many of them also which used curious arts brought their books together, and burned them before all *men*: and they counted the price of them, and found *it* fifty thousand *pieces* of silver" (Acts 19:19).

We must all understand that this is a real battle, and it must be fought daily. If in any way you participated in any of these things in the past, you can simply close the door by coming to Christ or renewing your covenant with Him through a rededication of your life and continuation in earnest, agonizing prayer.

This brings us to the next important question: What are the various strategies the devil uses today against the people of God?

The Wiles of Satan

"Finally, my brethren, be strong in the Lord, and in the power of his might. Put on the whole armour of God that ye may be able to stand against the wiles of the devil" (Eph. 6:10, 11). Here the Bible talks about the wiles of the devil. What is a wile? A wile is defined as a stratagem or magic spell intended to ensnare, beguile, playfully trick, deceive, skillfully outwit, or deceitfully entice somebody in order to get a desired benefit or manipulatively make somebody behave in a particular way. There are many wiles of the devil today, and we must not be ignorant of them. The Bible says, "Know ye not that they which run in a race run all, but one receiveth the prize? So run, that ye may obtain" (1 Cor. 9:24).

In this race, God has given each of us the right and opportunity to win. As the devil has now put all his genius to work, and as all the demons, billions of them, go to work overtime, "He is intruding his presence in every department of the household, in every street of our cities, in the churches, in the national councils, in the courts of justice, perplexing, deceiving, seducing, everywhere ruining the souls and bodies of men, women, and children, breaking up families, sowing hatred, emulation, strife, sedition, murder" (White 1911, p. 508).

We need to be absolutely vigilant at all cost. The Bible says, "Ye are of God, little children, and have overcome them: because greater is he that is in you, than he that is in the world" (1 John 4:4). Please listen carefully. Our enemy is limited in power. He is not all-powerful. He can only operate with the leeway we give him. That's why it is stated, "Don't give place to the devil" (Eph. 4:27). In other words, don't offer the devil any room to work in your life. Before we begin dissecting, in detailed analysis, the wiles of the enemy, let's first look at the crucial concept of evil days.

The Evil Days

"Wherefore take unto you the whole armour of God that ye may be able to withstand in the evil day, and having done all, to stand" (Eph. 6: 13). First of all, may I ask which day is an evil day? "Remember now thy Creator in the days of thy youth, while the evil days come not, nor the years draw nigh, when thou shalt say, I have no pleasure in them" (Eccles. 12:1).

The term "evil days" is a reference to days of limited privileges and opportunities in our lives. Evil days could be days we can no longer do things the way we are used to, either as a result of sickness, old age, financial handicap, or trials. And that is the day the devil and his angels operate with an intensified energy against us; it is a day or time in our lives when we are subject to the most severe temptations of the enemy.

It is the day when sudden and unlooked-for calamity, bereavement, unexpected sickness, or anguish brings our souls face to face with death, and the true inward character is revealed. Then "It will be made manifest whether or not there is any real faith in the promises of the word of God. It will be made manifest whether or not the soul is sustained by grace, whether there is oil in the vessel with the lamp" ("Have You Oil in Your Vessels With Your Lamps?" *The Review and Herald*, September 17, 1895).

There are two conditions that can bring one into this experience. The first condition is when we are living in sin, and the Lord withdraws His protection from us for a while and allows us to be tried. The Bible describes it this way: "I will be his father, and he shall be my son. If he commits iniquity, I will chasten him with the rod of men and with the stripes of the children of men" (2 Sam. 7:14).

This is called the chastening of the Lord. This is a period every child of God has to, in his or her experience, go through life's trails. "Trials and obstacles are the Lord's chosen methods of discipline and His appointed conditions of success.... The Lord allows His chosen ones to be placed in the furnace of affliction to prove what temper they are of and whether they can be fashioned for His work" (White 1905, p. 471).

The second condition is a test of faith, like the case of Job. Even though God testified that Job was a perfect man, yet He permitted the devil to try him. This trial is called the trial of faith. One may ask, 'Why would God allow His faithful ones to go through such ordeals?' The answer is that it is in a crisis moment that our true characters are revealed; when a sudden and unanticipated calamity overwhelms us; when we are brought face to face with death; that's when we show whether we are sustained by grace.

Contend with Hindrances

> But the prince of the kingdom of Persia withstood me one and twenty days: but, lo, Michael, one of the chief princes, came to help me; and I remained there with the kings of Persia… Then said he, Knowest thou wherefore I come unto thee? and now will I return to fight with the prince of Persia: and when I am gone forth, lo, the prince of Grecia shall come. (Daniel 10:13, 20)

In the furnace of trial, we are purified from the dross that prevents us from reflecting the image of Christ. God measures every trial and watches the fire that must test every soul

By this we see that heavenly agencies have to contend with hindrances before the purpose of God is fulfilled in its time. The king of Persia was controlled by the highest of all evil angels. He refused, as did Pharaoh, to obey the word of the Lord. Gabriel declared, He withstood me twenty-one days by his representations against the Jews. But Michael came to his help, and then he remained with the kings of Persia, holding the powers in check, giving right counsel against evil counsel. Good and evil angels are taking a part in the planning of God in His earthly kingdom. It is God's purpose to carry forward His work in correct lines, in ways that will advance His glory. But Satan is ever trying to counterwork God's purpose. Only by humbling themselves before God can God's servants advance His work. Never are they to depend on their own efforts or on outward display for success. (White, *The SDA Bible Commentary*, vol. 4, p. 1173)

The heavenly agencies have to contend with these hindrances today before the purpose of God is fulfilled in its time. This is part of His refining process, though it's hard for human nature to endure, but only by it can the dross be purged from the character. In the furnace of trial, we are purified from the dross that prevents us from reflecting the image of Christ. God measures every trial and watches the fire that must test every soul.

The Fiery Darts

"Above all, taking the shield of faith, wherewith ye shall be able to quench all the fiery darts of the wicked" (Eph. 6:16). The word "fiery" was originally derived from the Greek word *puroo*, which means "inflamed, burning fire, a conflagration." The word "dart" is from the Greek *belos*, which means "missile," so when we put the two words together, the image this will convey is an explosive missile. Therefore, every satanic projection is likened to a devastating missile, and this includes thought projection, incitement of feelings into frenzy, the awakening of animal passions, and indulgence of appetite.

Thought Projections

Thought projection is one of the enemy's most deadly weapons. Because his greatest ambition is to shipwreck the faith of believers, that's why He has put more effort into matching his power against the power of Christ by way of counteracting the influence of the Holy Spirit in the thought pattern of every believer. Here are some of the ways he attacks us today:

1. He tries to pollute the spiritual atmosphere around every believer with his foul spirit. When a Christian does not recognize the devil's presence and resist him immediately through agonizing prayer, he carries out his second attack.
2. He drains out the spiritual life of the believer and leaves him or her spiritually dry and empty. The believer will no longer find joy in holiness, personal Bible study, or communion with God. Every spiritual thing becomes a discordant note to the person. At this point, the enemy stages the third attack.
3. He now tries to take control of the mind. It is interesting to note that the first two attacks were aimed at counteracting the influence of the Holy Spirit in the life of the believer. Satan was successful because the believer was not on guard or conscious of his presence. With a lack of resistance, he takes control of the heart and now sits in the place of God. That's why the Bible says, "Keep thy heart with all diligence; for out of it *are* the issues of life" (Prov. 4:23).

Satan knows that if he takes control of the heart, he has now obtained the entry permit into one's life and can direct the destiny. Thought projection is a very confidential aspect of the subtle, manipulative power of darkness against people. Generally, this is a process of projecting certain thoughts to a person, who may be quickened to manifest such thoughts through actions.

Consequently, thoughts can be transferred from one mind to another on a subconscious level, not only when someone is around you, but even regardless of distance. And on a conscious level, this is used for subtle demonic manipulation. In other words, through an advanced occult process, psychic forces of diverse thoughts are projected in motion to strike and possess people and thus subject them to the lowest ebb of being.

Satan's greatest ambition is to control our minds. Every minute of the day he projects thoughts and tries to guide our imaginations and rule our lives. Paul's admonition is that we must be "Casting down imaginations, and every high thing that exalteth itself against the knowledge of God, and bringing into captivity every thought to the obedience of Christ;" (2 Cor. 10:5). Because God knows what the enemy will accomplish when he takes control of our minds, that's why we are warned, "Wherefore gird up the loins of your mind" (1 Peter 1:13).

Incitement of the Feelings

Incitement of the feelings into a frenzy is one of Satan's explosive missiles. Satan always wants us to lose control of our feelings and emotions. He wants to bring us into temporal madness. That is one of his greatest desires—to bring us into a condition where we cannot control our behavior, especially anger. Solomon wrote, "Be not hasty in thy spirit to be angry: for anger resteth in the bosom of fools" (Eccles. 7:9).

Writing to Ephesians, the apostle Paul states, "Let all bitterness, and wrath, and anger, and clamour, and evil speaking, be put away from you, with all malice: And be ye kind one to another, tenderhearted, forgiving one another, even as God for Christ's sake hath forgiven you" (Eph. 4:31–32).

If we must receive the latter rain, as brethren we must endeavor to put away differences amongst ourselves and come into unity and harmony. Those who continue the strife and backbiting that we see in many places today will not receive it.

The Bible says, "Now the works of the flesh are manifest, which are *these*; Adultery, fornication, uncleanness, lasciviousness, Idolatry, witchcraft, hatred, variance, emulations, wrath, strife, seditions, heresies, Envyings, murders, drunkenness, revellings" (Gal. 5:19–21).

How are personal conflicts or private offenses between church members to be settled? "Moreover if thy brother shall trespass against thee, go and tell him his fault between thee and him alone: if he shall hear thee, thou hast gained thy brother" (Matt. 18:15).

"A tender spirit, a gentle and winning deportment, may save the erring and hide a multitude of sins. God requires us to have that charity that 'suffereth long, and is kind'" (White, *Testimonies to the Church,* vol. 4, p. 65.2).

"But if he will not hear [thee, then] take with thee one or two more, that in the mouth of two or three witnesses every word may be established. And if he shall neglect to hear them, tell [it] unto the church: but if he neglect to hear the church, let him be unto thee as a heathen man and a publican" (Matt. 18:15–20).

How are church members to resolve personal issues that do not require disciplinary action? "How is it that when you have something against another Christian, you "go to law" and ask a heathen court to decide the matter instead of taking it to other Christians to decide which of you is right? Don't you know that some day we Christians are going to judge and govern the world? So why can't you decide even these little things among yourselves? ...So you should be able to decide your problems down here on earth easily enough" (1 Cor. 6:1–3, TLNT).

> "The question of forgiveness needs no interpretation. There is never a time or place where it is right for you or for me to say, 'I will not forgive my brother; I will not walk in fellowship with him.' He who does this places himself in opposition to the teachings of Christ. If your brother does you an injustice ignorantly, and then holds out the hand of fellowship, saying, "If I have erred, and have done you an injury, forgive me," and you draw away from him, refusing to forgive, you walk away from the great Counselor, and need yourself to repent and be forgiven. (White, *The Southern Watchman,* January 1, 1903, par. 4)

The Bible says, "Take heed to yourselves: If thy brother trespass against thee, rebuke him; and if he repent, forgive him. And if he trespass against thee seven times in a day, and seven times in a day turn again to thee, saying, I repent; thou shalt forgive him" (Luke 17:3–4).

"If he [a brother] does you an injury knowingly, and afterward repents, saying, 'Forgive me,' it is not for you to turn away, refusing to forgive him because you think that he does not feel humble enough and does not mean what he says. You have no right to judge him, because you cannot read the heart (White, *The Southern Watchman,* January 1, 1903, par. 5).

"If a brother errs, forgive him if he asks you. If he is not humble enough to ask, forgive him in your heart, and express your forgiveness in word and act. Then his sin will not in any degree rest on you. 'Consider thyself, lest thou also be tempted.' 'If he trespass against thee seven times in a day, and seven times in a day turn again to thee, saying, I repent, thou shalt forgive him.' And we are not only to forgive seven times, but seventy times seven. Just as often as God forgives us, we are to forgive one another" (White, *The Southern Watchman,* January 1, 1903, par. 6).

"One man is never to say to another, 'When I see that you have reformed, then I will forgive you.' This is not God's plan. This is in accordance with the promptings of human nature. By showing that you do not desire fellowship with your brother, you not only hurt his soul and your own, but you also wound and bruise the heart of Christ" (White, *Review and Herald,* April 8, 1902, par. 4).

Awakening of Animal Passion

In this satanic missile, there are five propensities that he uses to advance his attack on God's people: lust, lasciviousness, sex, a spirit of drowsiness, and indulgence of the appetite. The first three are among the most sadistic weapons that demonic forces use to manipulate the children of humanity and dominate and control their thoughts, words, and deeds.

> The animal passions, cherished and indulged, become very strong in this age, and untold evils in the marriage life are the sure results. In the place of the mind being developed and having the controlling power, the animal propensities rule over the higher and nobler powers until they are brought into subjection to the animal propensities. What is the result? Women's delicate organs are worn out and become diseased; childbearing is no more safe; sexual privileges are abused. Men are corrupting their own bodies, and the wife has become a bed servant to their inordinate, base lusts until there is no fear of God before their eyes. To indulge impulse that degrades both body and soul is the order of the marriage life. (White, *Mind, Character, and Personality,* vol. 1, p. 225)

Whenever people are under the control of these evil propensities, they will be daily manipulated by the powers of darkness, and such people can be destroyed at any moment. It is only when true believers remain subject to Christ's authority that they can overcome the forces of evil. The Scripture says, "There is therefore now no condemnation to them which are in Christ Jesus, who walk not after the flesh, but after the Spirit. For the law of the Spirit of life in Christ Jesus hath made me free from the law of sin and death" (Rom. 8:1, 2). Those who receive Christ are given the power to become the sons and daughters of God, and this power is the power of holiness and authority to live and move as His children. This is the highest authority that an individual can have in this universe. It is only such believers with such power and authority who overcomes the forces of darkness.

Sex in the Right Context

"Nevertheless he that standeth stedfast in his heart, having no necessity, but hath power over his own will, and hath so decreed in his heart that he will keep his virgin, doeth well" (1 Corinthians 7:37). A virgin is someone who has never had any sex. It is interesting to note that for a maiden, virginity is her special endowment from God. To fully grasp God's vision of virginity and sexuality in marriage, we need to consider the following insight.

Have you ever wondered why God placed in every woman a membrane of blood called a hymen? Why is there such a breakable tissue full of blood that spills away when it is broken? Without a doubt, the hymen is a gate. It was God who set that blood-filled vessel there as a covenant, sign, and token between the bearer and whoever mates with her. The Bible says, "Marriage *is* honourable in all, and the bed undefiled" (Hebrew 13:4).

Deflowering the virginity of a maiden was designed by God to always be after marriage. It is a solemn covenant struck and confirmed by the blood shed on that day. This is His way of saying, "Whoever enters into this woman shall only be able to do so by making a blood covenant to be joined to her for the rest of her life, from this point onward.

"If a man find a damsel *that is* a virgin, which is not betrothed, and lay hold on her, and lie with her, and they be found; Then the man that lay with her shall give unto the damsel's father fifty *shekels* of silver, and she shall be his wife; because he hath humbled her, he may not put her away all his days" (Deut. 22:28, 29).

It is little wonder that sexual intercourse was designed by God to take place only after the marriage contract is sealed between a man and a woman. As a matter of fact, what happens the first time a lady has sex is not just sex, but an immersion and bathing of the man with her hymen blood to initiate a covenant that is highly recognized in the spiritual realms of both light and darkness.

Sexual Perversions

Dear friends, I wish to have you fully understand the evil of sexual perversion, which is defined as abnormal or unacceptable sexual behavior. Sexual perversion includes the following:

1. Adultery—voluntary sexual intercourse between a married person and a person who is not the spouse.
2. Bisexuality—sexual attraction to both men and women.
3. Bestiality— sexual intercourse between a person and an animal.
4. Cunnilingus—stimulation of the female genitals using the tongue or lips.
5. Fornication—sexual intercourse between unmarried partners.
6. Fellatio—oral stimulation of a man's penis with the mouth.
7. Homosexual—sexual attraction to one's own gender.
8. Incest— sexual relations between people of the same family (by blood; even by marriage).
9. Lesbian—a homosexual woman.
10. Masturbation—stimulating one's own genitals with the hand for sexual pleasure.
11. Pederasty—sexual intercourse between a man and a boy.
12. Rape—forced sexual intercourse (one person not consenting to the other).
13. Pornography—visual material stimulating sexual desire.
14. Lasciviousness—feeling or revealing an overt sexual desire.
15. Transgender—A person who surgically changes genders.

The above sexual perversions and practices are what the Scripture described as inordinate affection. God created our sexual capacities. He knows best the conditions under which those capacities should be used so that they bring lasting satisfaction to all involved. That's why His Word has left us with the following warning: "Mortify therefore your members which are upon the earth; fornication, uncleanness, inordinate affection, evil concupiscence, and covetousness, which is idolatry: For which things' sake the wrath of God cometh on the children of disobedience" (Col. 3:5, 6).

Masturbation and Health

Masturbation is the act of having sex with oneself. In other words, this is self-fornication, which biblically goes against the original plan that

God had for sex. Masturbation poses health implications. According to Steven Fowkes, an organic chemist, consultant, nanotechnologist, and writer, "you lose selenium and zinc" when you ejaculate (http://1ref.us/qs, [accessed 11/15/2018]).

"Masturbation depletes the body of zinc, selenium, B-complex vitamins, as well as many other vital nutrients. Male and female sexual fluids are particularly rich in certain forms of zinc and selenium that are hard to replace with food and impossible to replace with supplements" (SexualReboot, http://1ref.us/r2, [accessed 11/15/2018]).

It is interesting to note that zinc is essential to every man because it is one of the primary minerals that produce testosterone, the hormone that promotes muscle growth and helps every man to feel masculine. The more a man masturbates, the more zinc he loses and the less testosterone he will have. However, when a man and woman have intercourse, the female compensates, with her vaginal secretion, for the loss of zinc and other minerals that the man lost during ejaculation. This is one indication that God's marvelous design is that sex should be between a male and female that are married, and not in any other form or scenario.

Masturbation always stimulates a part of a man's synthetic nervous system that gives him hormonal imbalance. When it's frequent, one suffers back pains, headaches, eye pain, blurriness, and even loss of vision. It's interesting to note that millions of young people are crippled by this tool that Satan is using to chain the minds of believers and non-believers alike.

The Sins of the LGBT

The sins of the LGBT (Lesbian, Gay, Bisexual, and Transgender) originated from the pit of hell to pull humanity down. The Bible says:

> Because that, when they knew God, they glorified *him* not as God, neither were thankful; but became vain in their imaginations, and their foolish heart was darkened. Professing themselves to be wise, they became fools… Wherefore God also gave them up to uncleanness through the lusts of their own hearts, to dishonour their own bodies between themselves… For this cause God gave them up unto vile affections: for even their women did change the natural use into that which is against nature… And likewise also the men, leaving the natural use of the woman, burned in their lust one toward another… And even as they did not like to retain God in *their* knowledge, God gave them over to a reprobate mind, to do those things which are not convenient. (Romans 1:22–28)

Let me say once more that manipulations through sexual acts are the most effective tools used in demonic operations against people, to pull them down to a low spiritual ebb.

> When we speak of low spiritual ebb, we are speaking of a state in which the life of a person is subjected to the lowest degree of the spiritual scale of being. In this repugnant state, an individual can be controlled, managed, dominated, or manipulated by the forces of darkness even beyond his or her awareness.
>
> Sexual perversion is the highest secret power used in all ramifications of occult and psychic manipulations to dominate and control the thoughts, words, and deeds of the people of this world. In advanced vicious psychic operations, sexual act is like fuel while lust is like fire. Therefore, as constant supply of fuel can never extinguish fire, so no amount of sexual act can extinguish lust. (Uzorma, *Occult Grand Master Now in Christ*, vol. 1, p. 44)

God's Word admonishes, "Flee fornication. Every sin that a man doeth is without the body; but he that committeth fornication sinneth against his own body" (1 Cor. 6:18). As our world moves into its last phase in history, the powers of darkness now manipulate every activity of a carnal person to revolve around sexual perversion.

"The true Christian will not desire to enter any place of amusement or engage in any diversion upon which he cannot ask the blessing of God. He will not be found at the theater, the billiard hall, or the bowling saloon. He will not unite with the gay waltzers or indulge in any other bewitching pleasure that will banish Christ from the mind" (White 1952, pp. 515, 516).

Indulgence of Appetite

The indulgence of appetite is one of the weapons the enemy of human souls uses to attack us physically and spiritually. It strengthens the animal propensities in us and weakens our power to resist perverse orgies. It blunts the nobler sentiments of the mind. These appetites were given to us for good, necessary purposes, not to become the ministers of death through perversion.

The appetite for tobacco, hard drugs, alcohol, a flesh diet, and gluttony distorts our spiritual life. Therefore, God requires of every human being cooperation with Him, that none may go beyond the proper boundary in overeating or partaking of improper articles of food. The whole being is degraded, and the human agent becomes the slave of appetite by pampering and indulging one's own groveling sensual passions.

Overcrowding the stomach weakens the mind and produces forgetfulness and loss of memory. Overeating blunts the emotions. The intellectual, moral, and physical powers are depreciated by the habitual use of flesh meats. Meat-eating deranges the system, beclouds the intellect, and blunts the moral sensibilities. God desires us, by strict temperance, to keep our minds clear and keen, that we may be able to distinguish between the sacred and the common. We should strive to understand the wonderful science of the matchless compassion and benevolence of God.

Those who eat too excessively and/or unhealthful foods bring trouble upon themselves, unfitting themselves for the service of God. It is dangerous to eat meat, for animals are suffering from many deadly diseases. Those who persist in eating the flesh of animals sacrifice themselves to a perverted appetite. Their bodies become full of disease.

These are ways the devil tries to take us captive, but by faith, we can resist him. Faith is the spiritual hand that touches infinity. It is the medium by which the renewed heart is made to beat in unison with the heart of Christ. Faith looks beyond the difficulties and lays hold of the unseen. The wheel of faith carries us along this road of sanctification to the heights of victory.

> *These are ways the devil tries to take us captive, but by faith, we can resist him. Faith is the spiritual hand that touches infinity. It is the medium by which the renewed heart is made to beat in unison with the heart of Christ*

What Is Temperance?

Temperance is defined as abstinence from that which is harmful and moderating that which is good. While intemperance is a lack of self-control, characterized by excessive indulgence, appetite, and overeating, it is seen in the quantity and quality of food eaten.

> Intemperance embraces much. With some it consists of eating too largely of food which, if taken in proper quantities, would not be objectionable. All that is taken into the stomach above the actual need of the system becomes a dangerous element. It decays in the stomach, and causes dyspepsia. Continual overeating uses up the vital forces, and deprives the brain of power to do its work....

...Those who are not health reformers treat themselves unfairly and unwisely. By the indulgence of appetite they do themselves fearful injury. Some may think that the question of diet is not important enough to be included in the question of religion. But such make a great mistake. God's word declares, "Whether therefore ye eat, or drink, or whatsoever ye do, do all to the glory of God." (White, *Temperance*, pp. 162, 163)

Learning to eat properly and control the innate appetite within us are spiritual matters. It, therefore, requires the application of spiritual truth and use of spiritual weapons. "It is of great importance that individually we act well our part, and have an intelligent understanding of what we should eat and drink, and how we should live to preserve health. All are being proved to see whether they will accept the principles of health reform or follow a course of self-indulgence" (White 1949, p. 163).

CHAPTER 5

THE JOURNEY OF RECOVERY

Many years ago, a man wrote the following letter to his younger brother to awaken him to the far-reaching power of his habits.

My dear brother,

Some of the subjects upon which I intend to address you, will perhaps seem small. Nothing is small, however, or unimportant, which concerns the forming of your habits. You are now forming a character for life, and ten years hence it will be too late to amend what is done amiss now.

Near the place where I write, a number of men are busied in building a large house. They are building up thick walls of solid stone. Now I observe that they are very careful in laying these stones. They are constantly measuring with the rule and the plummet, to make every part exactly as it should be. And they have reason for this, because, if, six months hence, they should find out that their wall was not perpendicular, or their foundation not strong, they could do nothing to remedy it—but to tear down their work and do it over again.

So it is with you. Every habit you form is one stone laid in your character....

...True religion, I know, works great and happy changes in some, even late in life. But what I desire for you is, that religion may work this change early in life or rather that the grace of God may so mold your character now, that in these particulars there may be no need of a change so radical. For it is better to lay the foundation right at the beginning, than to tear down the whole walls to put right what is found to be wrong. (My Brother's Keeper, http://1ref.us/qt, [accessed 11/15/2018])

There are several vital points of truth in this abridged letter that are applicable to our lives. Our homes, families, the lives we live, friends we keep, and habits often tend to forge or decide our eternal destiny. Have you ever thought about this? In every life, there's always a path that flows through adversity. Often such adversity can be God's call to us for self-examination, and more importantly motivation for us to cry out to Him. May I take you through a journey into my world and share some experiences?

My Childhood Identity

Born into the humble family of a peasant farmer in Nigeria, I was raised under the care of a single mother who experienced lots of difficulty in childbearing and lost many babies through child epidemics. Very apprehensive and worried if her only son could survive the epidemic of that time, she thought, 'What if death takes him away at a tender age just as it has with my other babies?' It was this foreboding that led to her determination to have a second male child to compliment the first.

Our homes, families, the lives we live, friends we keep, and habits often tend to forge or decide our eternal destiny

She had another son on April 1, 1976. This baby boy was born amidst shouts of joy and jubilation. And this child was me. After my birth, my mother visited a voodoo priest to carry out some rituals in line with African voodoo traditions.

At seven years old, I began having a particularly vivid nightmare which I felt wasn't just a nightmare. Usually, I would dream of seeing a black figure standing next to my bed. When I would try to move or call out for help, I always found myself paralyzed in what may look like sleep paralysis, and my skin always got cut with sharp objects, and this left me with bleeding surface marks.

Some other strange experiences I constantly witnessed or noticed around me were cats and owls, at a particular hour of the night, would come by the side of my window and make strange noises. I would notice that after I just woke up in the morning from the bed, my face and head was caught up in a cobweb. Even when others in the house had passed the place already, when it came to my turn, my face and head were caught in the cobweb.

Sometimes it happened along the road, where people were moving in front of me. My face was caught in the cobweb. It happened to me anywhere and at any time of the day. It was very strange, but I typically didn't read any meaning into it. I just brushed it away as mere coincidence.

However, let's analyze something here. Regarding the times it happened outside along the street or in an open field, it's quite impossible for a spider to spin its web in a place where there are no visible support or connection points. Also, how fast can it spin a web when others had passed through the same place a few seconds before I was caught in it?

This experience continued into my adulthood, and I was really disturbed, so I began asking questions and seeking to understand why such an experience was happening to me. Who was responsible?

> I saw that the enemy will contend either for the usefulness or the life of the godly, and will try to mar their peace as long as they live in this world. But his power is limited. He may cause the furnace to be heated, but Jesus and angels will watch the trusting Christian, that nothing may be consumed but the dross. The fire kindled by Satan can have no power to destroy or hurt the true metal. It is important to close every door possible, against the entrance of Satan. It is the privilege of every family so to live that Satan can take no advantage of anything they may say or do, to tear one another down. Every member of the family should bear in mind that all have just as much as they can do to resist our wily foe, and with earnest prayers and unyielding faith each must rely upon the merits of the blood of Christ and claim His saving strength. (White, *Testimonies for the Church*, vol. 1, p. 309)

I noticed a power was aggressively contending for my usefulness, preventing me from being fruitful, attacking my spiritual growth, arresting my progress, subjecting me to stagnation and retrogression, trying to substitute success with failure, and making advancement difficult to achieve. High-voltage spiritual snares were set as traps on my path. Sometimes I would notice that the spiritual atmosphere around my soul was polluted with a foul spirit, as a bewitching spell was cast upon my soul, and the enemy of my soul was seen trying to alienate me from God. I found myself struggling with the spirit of addiction to appetite and sexual perversion. Do you know that inspiration also reveals this?

> The powers of darkness gather about the soul and [try to] shut Jesus from our sight, and at times we can only wait in sorrow and amazement until the cloud passes over. These seasons are sometimes terrible. Hope seems to fail, and despair seizes upon us. In these dreadful hours we

must learn to trust, to depend solely upon the merits of the atonement, and in all our helpless unworthiness cast ourselves upon the merits of the crucified and risen Saviour. We shall never perish while we do this--*never*! When light shines on our pathway, it is no great thing to be strong in the strength of grace. But to wait patiently in hope when clouds envelop us and all is dark, requires faith and submission which causes our will to be swallowed up in the will of God. We are too quickly discouraged, and earnestly cry for the trial to be removed from us, when we should plead for patience to endure and grace to overcome. (White, *Testimonies for the Church*, vol. 1, pp. 309, 310)

This may sound like a fairytale. Most would label it as a creative, fictitious, and surreal account of supernatural experiences, not to be taken literally. However, this is a real and true experience. I also had this personal encounter with satanic influences, so I know that it is true. It is time we recognize the reality of satanic manipulation in the spiritual realm and begin to correct this deficiency at once. The information contained in this story is an account of my spiritual struggle and victory.

Adolescent Experiment

Though from my adolescence I began fully participating in church activities, my religion was just a mere formality. My life was ruled by the sins of temper, resentment, irritation, impatience, strife, and lust. In my early stage of life, I cultivated the evil habit of masturbation. I remember clearly, and with inexpressible regret, how I entangled myself in the use of pornography. One glance at that sexual image sent a rush through my system very much like a narcotic response.

The longer I gazed, the more intoxicated I became, and over the next few hours, the image brought me temporal escape and exhilaration. Now I had found a new drug, and it seemed to work beyond my expectations. As I glanced through these filthy images, I spiraled into masturbation, and as I grew, the urge and desire grew with me.

With that said, deep in my heart, I loved the things pertaining to God. The beautiful stories I heard and read in my teens made some profound impressions in my heart. However, the strength in me to resist sinful propensities is weak, and my heart is carnal, filled with fantasies and lustful imagination.

Age of Responsibility

Now as a full-grown young man, my utmost desire was to be successful and progressive in every area of my life, but this experience seemed to elude me. I noticed that my ways were hedged up in all directions. Nothing seemed to be working, and I could not tell what was responsible.

The general notion is that as long as one goes to church, reads the Bible, knows the truth, goes out to evangelize, fully participates in church activities, and is called by the name "Christian," the devil has no power over such a person. In fact, such a notion gave some sense of false security, a security which did not really exist, considering the fact that in my lifestyle I never cared about the impure and immoral music to which I listened, videos and TV shows I watched, books and magazines I read, especially with some phonographic imagery bombarding my youthful mind, or my addictions to masturbation and competitive sports. In spite of all these, I zealously participated in church activities and convinced myself that I was a Christian by those works.

What a great deception, thinking you're right with God because you're involved in church activities when you live an unconverted life and temper, resentment, irritation, impatience, strife, and lust control you. I also had not known the need for a death to self and sin or the import of the work of the Holy Spirit to regenerate the heart. The fundamental consideration of every soul should be, 'Is my heart renewed? Is my soul transformed? Are my sins pardoned through faith in Christ? Have I been born again?'

Can I Be Victorious?

God's Word reveals that "Without faith it is impossible to please God. We can have the salvation of God in our families, but we must believe it, live for it, and have a continual, abiding faith and trust in God" (White 1868, p. 310). When I understood that I could overcome through faith and that my habits were indeed very powerful and highly consequential to my destiny, spirituality, aptitudes, and altitudes, then my utmost and desperate desire was to practically seek to obtain victory over my perverse way of life.

> We must subdue a hasty temper and control our words, and in this we shall gain great victories. Unless we control our words and temper, we are slaves to Satan. We are in subjection to him. He leads us captive. All jangling and unpleasant, impatient, fretful words are an offering presented to his Satanic majesty. And it is a costly offering, more costly than any sacrifice we can make for God, for it destroys the peace and happiness of whole families, destroys health, and is eventually the cause of forfeiting an eternal life of happiness. (White, *Testimonies for the Church*, vol. 1, p. 310)

Realizing this, I then sat down and wrote down on a plain sheet of paper all the sins that easily beset my soul. I earnestly sought God through prayers, asking for a total conversion in which I found Him in an experience that changed me.

> The restraint which God's word imposes upon us is for our own interest. It increases the happiness of our families and of all around us. It refines our taste, sanctifies our judgment, and brings peace of mind, and, in the end, everlasting life. Under this holy restraint we shall increase in grace and humility, and it will become easy to speak right. The natural, passionate temper will be held in subjection. An indwelling Saviour will strengthen us every hour. Ministering angels will linger in our dwellings and with joy carry heavenward the tidings of our advance in the divine life, and the recording angel will make a cheerful, happy record. (White, *Testimonies for the Church*, vol. 1, p. 310)

From thence all I lived for was to please the Lord. My eyes were continually turned towards Him, and in the wonder of this new-birth experience, I found victory over sin. However, as the days passed by, the victorious life once again became more of a struggle, iniquity began to conquer me again more frequently, and the Christian life became more of an uphill climb. I prayed, studied, fought, and repented, and sometimes I would truly rediscover the beauty of that earlier experience, but with an aching heart, I would notice that this did not remain with me for more than a few days. Then the bitter struggle and defeats would begin again.

My sins were not open sins; they are secret sins, such as temper, resentment, irritation, impatience, strife, and lust. Though publicly I was respected and appeared to hate sin with all my heart, something inside me mocked me and continued to master my thoughts, desires, motives, and feelings. I convinced myself that these inward and secret pollutions were not so dangerous as long as I did not allow them to come out, but that was impossible. At unwary moments they would reveal themselves and prove that inwardly there was corruption.

Even when I managed to restrain these inward impulses, my conscience condemned me, and each morning or at the end of each day, my prayer was often focused on the confession of sins committed. I knew something was missing in my life. I knew that there was a better way because, first, I remembered my former experience, and second, I knew the New Testament teaches that the life of the born-again Christian is a life of victory.

Texts such as the following burned into my heart like a firebrand each time I read them, and they kept me seeking: "For sin shall not have dominion over you: for ye are not under the law, but under grace" (Rom. 6:14). "Whosoever abideth in him sinneth not: whosoever sinneth hath not seen him, neither known him" (1 John 3:6).

In addition to these texts and many others, the testimonies of the apostles of Christ were that they lived victorious lives. They were not slaves to sin but conquerors in the strength of Christ. Paul could say, "For I know nothing by myself; yet am I not hereby justified: but he that judgeth me is the Lord" (1 Cor. 4:4). "I have fought a good fight, I have finished *my* course, I have kept the faith" (2 Tim. 4:7).

It is definitely the will of God that all His children should immediately overcome every sin and walk continuously in perfect victory as long as they live. Because of my secret sins, my life was empty, unhappy, painful, emotionally struggling, troubling, arduous, and fraught with failure. I saw myself physically dying; my youthfulness and usefulness were seriously contested by the enemy of human souls. I longed for the purity and righteousness that, in myself, I was powerless to attain, and like Paul the apostle I cried out, "O wretched man that I am! who shall deliver me from this body of death" (Rom. 7:24)?

Diagnosis and Dialysis

Then one night, I had a most unusual dream that changed my life forever. In that dream, I saw a body lying on a couch without life. Efforts were made to resuscitate the person back to life. Suddenly a man appeared standing beside the lifeless body, diagnosing the actual cause of death. He said that this body was disconnected from the veritable spring of life, as well as intemperate in eating and drinking. After he said this, I suddenly woke up from my sleep.

Friends, do you know that when God gives us victory over sin, the lustful desires and propensities, though still in us, are subdued by Him? Christ gives us the power to subdue them daily. And for us to subdue our flesh daily, our devotion to and communion with God must be daily. Without a consistent devotional life, no soul can be saved.

The victory God gives is a daily victory. We have to subdue the flesh daily. Satan on the outside cannot affect us. The only thing he does is put temptation in front of us to cause us to lust for fleshly wants. If the flesh is weak, then we succumb to Satan's temptation. "Genuine sanctification … is nothing less than a daily dying to self and daily conformity to the will of God" (White 1952, p. 248). "It is the daily dying to self in the little transactions of life that makes us overcomers" (White 1967, p. 233).

Inspiration reveals that "A religious life can be more successfully gained and maintained if meat is discarded, for this diet stimulates into intense activities lustful propensities, and enfeebles the moral and spiritual nature. 'The flesh warreth against the spirit, and the spirit against the flesh'" (White 1926, p. 28).

Through this dream, I realized how wretched, blind, and naked I was and why I urgently needed Christ to abide in me and quicken my spirit and lifeless body. I also considered my diet—what, how, and when I eat—realizing that God does not only have an interest in my spiritual health, but also my mental and physical health. "What you need is less temporal food and much more spiritual food, more of the bread of life. The simpler your diet, the better it will be for you" (White 1938, p. 102).

Recognizing the actual course of my spiritual weakness, I sincerely cried out to God for mercy and rescue, confessing all the wrongs of the past, and genuinely accepted Christ into my heart. Pleading for His guidance and spiritual nurture, I asked Him to take me by hand, lead me along the path He wanted me to pursue, take control of my appetite, and transform my taste buds to His glory. I also asked for divine grace to recognize His voice when He speaks to me, as well as the power to obey every word that proceeds from His mouth.

My heart was so broken that I wept like one who has lost a loved one. While still on my knees, I began sensing an incomparable peace flooding my soul. I felt so light, like I could fly ten thousand miles. The determination to obey every command of the Lord immediately began settling in my mind.

I was now ready and willing to obey every word from both the Bible and Spirit of Prophecy without question. As my heart began to yield to the impression of the Holy Spirit, I added other prayer points:

Dear Lord, please seal up every doorway and avenue of satanic invasion into my life. Destroy the urges and propensities that have caused me to commit these sins and live in immoral ways. With tears, I ask God to open my eyes, that I may always see any backsliding in my life and give me the grace to maintain good standing with Him in purity and holiness.

Dear Lord, please help me to do my best. Teach me how to do better work. Give me energy and cheerfulness. Help me to bring into my service the loving ministry of our loving Savior. All this I ask through the merits of the precious blood of our Lord and Savior Jesus Christ. Amen.

My eyes were continually turned towards God. With a strong impression in me, I drew up the following one-week fruit-fasting diet pattern for myself and strictly followed it to the end.

S/N	DAY 1	DAILY MEAL	PRAYER TIME	MEAL TIME
1	BREAKFAST	MANGO	6:00 a.m.	6:15 a.m.
2	LUNCH	BANANAS, BLUEBERRIES, DATES AND ABOUT A CUP OF COCONUT MILK	noon	noon
3	DINNER	SOY MILK	6:00 p.m.	6:15 p.m.
	DAY 2	DAILY MEAL	PRAYER TIME	MEAL TIME
1	BREAKFAST	MANGO	6:00 a.m.	6:15 a.m.
2	LUNCH	A BOWL OF CHOPPED WATERMELON, CUCUMBER, AND BANANA	noon	noon
3	DINNER	SOY MILK	6:00 p.m.	6:15 p.m.
	DAY 3	DAILY MEAL	PRAYER TIME	MEAL TIME
1	BREAKFAST	A BOWL OF FRUIT SALAD, WITH BANANAS, APPLES, AND BERRIES	6:00 a.m.	6:15 a.m.
2	LUNCH	WHEAT BREAD/ BEANS	noon	noon
3	DINNER	SOY MILK	6:00 p.m.	6:15 p.m.
	DAY 4	DAILY MEAL	PRAYER TIME	MEAL TIME
1	BREAKFAST	PAPAYA AND PINEAPPLE BLENDED TOGETHER	6:00 a.m.	6:15 a.m.

2	LUNCH	GRANOLA/WHEAT BREAD	noon	noon
3	DINNER	SOY MILK	6:00 p.m.	6:15 p.m.
	DAY 5	**DAILY MEAL**	**PRAYER TIME**	**MEAL TIME**
1	BREAKFAST	SALAD OF FRESH VEGETABLES	6:00 a.m.	6:15 a.m.
2	LUNCH	APPLE JUICE	noon	noon
3	DINNER	SOY MILK	6:00 p.m.	6:15 p.m.
	DAY 6	**DAILY MEAL**	**PRAYER TIME**	**MEAL TIME**
1	BREAKFAST	WATERMELON JUICE	6:00 a.m.	6:15 a.m.
2	LUNCH	GRANOLA/WHEAT BREAD	noon	noon
3	DINNER	SOY MILK	6:00 p.m.	6:15 p.m.
	DAY 7	**DAILY MEAL**	**PRAYER TIME**	**MEAL TIME**
1	BREAKFAST	APPLE JUICE	6:00 a.m.	6:15 a.m.
2	LUNCH	WHEAT BREAD/ BEANS	noon	noon
3	DINNER	A BOWL OF CHOPPED WATERMELON, CUCUMBER, AND BANANA	6:00 p.m.	6:15 p.m.

I not only followed a strict diet pattern; I also crafted a consistent prayer pattern. I set apart special time for prayer each day, with four-hour intervals each season. I went to bed early every evening, at 8:00 p.m., with the plan to awake by 3:00 a.m. for prayer and Bible studies each morning until 6:00 a.m.

Indeed, this experience paid off. I felt the power of God in a way I never felt before. My diet drove down my high testosterone levels, calmed down my nerves, reinvigorated my health, and restored my youthfulness and soundness of mind.

> God demands that the appetite be cleansed, and that self-denial be practiced in regard to those things which are not good. This is a work that will have to be done before His people can stand before Him a perfected people….
>
> …There are those who ought to be awake to the danger of meat eating, who are still eating the flesh of animals, thus endangering the physical, mental, and spiritual health. Many who are now only half converted on the question of meat eating will go from God's people to walk no more with them. (White, *Counsels on Diet and Foods*, pp. 381, 382)

While more explicit sins were mainly the cause of my spiritual stagnation, the indulgence of appetite also contributed to my weakness. It was the cause of why nothing seemed to be working in my life. However, nobody seemed to be talking about this in a more practical way in the church; nobody seemed to be telling the youth that their success and breakthrough in life are dependent upon their relationship with Christ and resultant lifestyles. I stand this day to testify that God still changes lives.

Our Habits

Our habits are indeed very powerful and highly impact our destinies. They are those patterns of behavior in our lives that started as simple acts but, being often repeated, have become a part of us and even manifest subconsciously. This is not surprising as they are mostly the outcomes of the thoughts and emotional patterns systematically engraved on our minds.

As "little" as some of them appear, they have the potential to make or mar us, shape our lives, influence our reputations, and determine our destinies. In fact, our real strength and worth are not determined by how much wealth, fame, or education we have, but by the kinds of habits that govern our lives. The Bible says, "For he that soweth to his flesh shall of the flesh reap corruption; but he that soweth to the Spirit shall of the Spirit reap life everlasting" (Gal. 6:8).

However, with damaging habits, the beauty and glory of our spiritual lives are drained away, and the horizon of our happiness, fulfillment, and accomplishments is darkened. This is why we must pay close attention to the kinds of habits we develop in our lives.

Ensnaring Pursuits

The reason the spiritual lives of many Christians today seem so repulsively deformed is that they have become habitually conformed to the world rather than continually transformed by the Spirit of God. The Bible says, "And be not conformed to this world: but be ye transformed by the renewing of your mind, that ye may prove what *is* that good, and acceptable, and perfect, will of God" (Rom. 12:2).

We must neuter the habit of obsessive pursuits after riches, fame, power, pleasures, and other gilded toys of the world. "No man that warreth entangleth himself with the affairs of *this* life; that he may please him who hath chosen him to be a soldier" (2 Timothy 2:4). The world and the Lord are on divergent lines. The deeper we get entangled in the transient affairs and attractions of the world, the more we become alienated from God and His glory. The more we are preoccupied with the cares of the world, the more we assume its unregenerate nature and lose focus on heaven and the great commission. "Therefore take no thought, saying, What shall we eat? or, What shall we drink? or, Wherewithal shall we be clothed? (For after all these things do the Gentiles seek:) for your heavenly Father knoweth that ye have need of all these things" (Matt. 6:31, 32).

> *We must deal decidedly with the habit of engaging in entertainment that defiles our hearts, ruins our consciences, and renders us spiritually empty and dry. We must exercise temperance in all things*

Ungodly Amusements

These are the days of the proliferation of social and entertainment media in different forms and versions—worldly music, movies, reality shows, soap operas, competitive sports, games, the Internet, and so on, from the biggest of devices to the smallest of gadgets. Many who are ignorant of Satan's strategy in making the corrupting entertainment formats readily available and affordable have mortgaged the richness of their relationship with God as they become gradually addicted. We must deal decidedly with the habit of engaging in entertainment that defiles our hearts, ruins our consciences, and renders us spiritually empty and dry. We must exercise temperance in all things.

Knowing God's Will

You are at a dead end. And you just don't know which way to turn. You really want to know what you should do. Here you are faced with an important decision and you want to do what is right. You ask yourself a thousand times, *"What should I do?"* You pray about it, but somehow there does not seem to be an easy answer. Why is that? God does not hand us the ready-made answer on a platter. No, you are still faced with the struggle, *"Which way should I turn?"*

You ask yourself, *"How can I know what the Lord wants me to do?"* You talk to friends. One tells you one thing, and another tells you something else. You are confused, and you think some more. But the answer does not seem to come. How often have you been the one making this plea? So many times we find ourselves in such a distressing dilemma, searching for some help in evaluating an important life decision.

George Mueller was a very sincere and devout Christian man of God in Bristol, England. Shortly before his death in 1898, Mueller shared the basic principles he had found helpful in his efforts to know and follow God's will in making decisions in his own life.

Having read the Bible through approximately two hundred times, Mueller was so convinced from his reading of God's promises that if the "cattle of a thousand hills" belong to the Lord, and God is "our strength" and the "rewarder of them that diligently seek Him", then we should learn to depend upon Him rather than man.

Mueller testifies that all through his life he never, ever solicited funds from the public, from the church, or from others. He never had any fundraising campaigns. Whenever there was a need he got down on his knees and took it to the Lord, and the Lord provided.

There were many tests of faith, but he always stood steadfast. On one occasion, shortly after he had made this commitment with the Lord, a lady came to him and said, "Pastor, I understand that you need some money. How much do you need?" He responded, "My dear sister, I have made a commitment with the Lord that I would never reveal to others what the needs are, but that I would always take them to the Master."

Somewhat impatiently his caller said, "Well, the Lord has told me that you need some money and here it is." She gave him a sum of money that was precisely the amount that he needed to provide food for his orphans on that particular day.

It would be nice to have a large fund from which we could draw to carry on the Lord's work, but the Lord says, "No depend on Me and I will take care of your needs." That was pastor Mueller's experience. He kept meticulous records, and toward the end of his life he indicated that he had received over five thousand specific answers to his prayers.

Mueller shared the basic principles he had found helpful in his efforts to know and follow God's will in making decisions in his life. He testified that, in trivial matters and in transactions involving most important issues, he had found this method always effective.

I would like to share those principles with you, along with other inspired counsels from the Word of God. But first it would be well to look at what the Bible tells us the will of God is for us: "For this is the will of God, [even] your sanctification that ye should abstain from fornication" (1 Thess. 4:3).

Paul tells us that our sanctification is God's ultimate will and that's what underlines all of His dealings with us. Anything that does not tend towards our sanctification He does not approve. As Mueller sought to know the will of God, he tried as much as possible in every effort undertaken, even down to the smallest expenditure, to only proceed when he was certain he was in God's will. The following are his principles:

1. SUBMISSION TO GOD'S WILL

"I seek at the beginning to get my heart into such a state that it has no will of its own in regard to a given matter".

"Trust in the LORD with all thine heart; and lean not unto thine own understanding. In all thy ways acknowledge him, and he shall direct thy paths" (Prov. 3:5–6).

This step is generally the hardest of all. If we can get self out of the way, and completely place our will in God's will, a hundred percent of the difficulties are overcome. **"Jesus saith unto them, My meat is to do the will of him that sent me, and to finish his work"** (John 4:34).

Sister White tells us, "So utterly was Christ emptied of self that He made no plans for Himself. He accepted God's plans for Him, and day by day the Father unfolded His plans. So should we depend upon God, that our lives may be the simple outworking of His will" (White, *The Desire of Ages,* p. 208.2).

Jesus emptied Himself of His own will. He was the Creator. He was the one in charge of everything. He created you and me. Who else had more right to do whatever He wanted to do? But He said that He came "Not to do mine own [human] will, but the will of him [God] that sent me" (John 6:38). So "Let this mind be in you, which was also in Christ Jesus" (Phil. 2:5).

So then, what happens to us when our will merges with God's will? Inspiration reveals that, "As the will of man co-operates with the will of God, it becomes omnipotent. Whatever is to be done at His command may be accomplished in His strength. All His biddings are enabling" (White, *Christ's Object Lessons,* p. 333.1).

After we have placed our will in God's will, we can turn to Mueller's other principles:

2. DO NOT DEPEND ON FEELINGS

"Having done this, I do not leave the result to feeling or simple impressions. If so, I make myself liable to great delusions".

In other words, Mueller said he does not go by feeling and simple impressions or impulses for to do that is to lay oneself wide open to satanic delusion.

The servant of the Lord reveals this:

> I was shown that, as God revived His work, those who had formerly been in fanaticism would be in danger of crediting their **impressions and feelings**, and the devil would use them to push poor souls into the fire. Satan uses some as long as he can push souls into the waters (into cold formality), and then when he has accomplished all he wishes in that direction, he will give them a blind zeal and lead them to be moved by **feelings and impressions,** and through them will push souls into the fire to be consumed by fanaticism. (White, *Manuscript Releases,* vol. 11, p. 352.1)

There is one thing about our feelings, impressions, and emotions that is sure, and that is that they are going to change. "Your feelings, your impressions, your emotions, are not to be trusted, for they are not reliable" (White, *Testimonies for the Church,* vol. 5, p. 513).

"Delight thyself also in the LORD; and he shall give thee the desires of thine heart. Commit thy way unto the LORD; trust also in him; and he shall bring [it] to pass" (Ps. 37:4–5).

3. ANCHORED IN THE WORD

"I seek the will of the Spirit of God through or in connection with the Word of God. The Spirit and the Word must be combined. If I look to the Spirit alone without the Word, I lay myself open to great delusions also."

"Thy word [is] a lamp unto my feet and a light unto my path … Order my steps in thy word: and let not any iniquity have dominion over me" (Ps. 119:105, 133).

"Every soul must be regulated by the law of God. Compare everything you propose to do with the law of God. Ask, is this the way of the Lord?" (White, *The Ellen G. White 1888 Materials*, p. 1685).

Sister White also tells us,

> There are three ways in which the Lord reveals His will to us, to guide us. ... **God reveals His will to us in His word**, the Holy Scriptures; **His voice is also revealed in His providential workings**; and it will be recognized if we do not separate our souls from Him by walking in our own ways, doing according to our own wills, and following the promptings of an unsanctified heart ... Another **way, in which God's voice is heard, is through the appeals of His Holy Spirit**, making impressions upon the heart, which will be wrought out in the character. (White, *Messages to Young People,* p. 156.1–4)

4. PROVIDENTIAL CIRCUMSTANCE

"Next I take into account providential circumstances. These plainly indicate God's will in connection with His Word and Spirit".

Mueller said he tried to look back, reviewing past history, taking note of providential circumstances in every stage of his life. He would mark out each difficult path and show how God's miraculous dealings saw him through in his life in the ways and manner in which his prayers were answered.

"And thou shalt remember all the way which the LORD thy God led thee these forty years in the wilderness, to humble thee, [and] to prove thee, to know what [was] in thine heart, whether thou wouldest keep his commandments, or no" (Deut 8:2).

The servant of God expressed the same principle in words more familiar to us. She said, "We have nothing to fear for the future, except as we shall forget the way the Lord has led us and His teaching in our past history" (White, *Life Sketches of Ellen G. White,* p. 196.2).

5. PRAY FOR GUIDANCE

After going through all of these steps and taking into account all of these principles, Mueller stated his principle number five as, *"I ask God in prayer clearly to reveal His will to me."*

Moses also believed the same for he prayed, **"Now therefore, I pray thee, if I have found grace in thy sight, show me now thy way, that I may know thee, that I may find grace in thy sight"** (Ex. 33:13).

It is His will that we know Him, that we become so well acquainted with Him that we learn to think and act as He thinks and acts—that we may partake of His character:

And if we consent, He will so identify Himself with our thoughts and aims, so blend our hearts and minds into conformity to His will, that when obeying Him we shall be but carrying out our own impulses. The will, refined and sanctified, will find its highest delight in doing His service. When we know God as it is our privilege to know Him, our life will be a life of continual obedience. Through an appreciation of the character of Christ, through communion with God, sin will become hateful to us. (White, *The Desire of Ages,* p. 668.3)

How can we pray according to Christ's will? The Bible says, **"that whatsoever ye shall ask of the Father in my name, he may give it you"** (John 15:16).

Not only must we pray in Christ's name, but we must understand what that really means. "But to pray in Christ's name means much. It means that we are to accept His character, manifest His spirit, and work His works" (White, *The Desire of Ages,* p. 668).

6. DECIDE

Mueller stated his principle number six in these words, *"Through prayer to God, the study of the Word, and reflection, I come to a deliberate judgment according to the best of my ability and knowledge, and if my mind is thus at peace, and continues so after two or three more petitions, I proceed accordingly. In trivial matters and in transactions involving most important issues, I have found this method always effective."*

What he is saying is that after all this prayerful consideration, he finally came to a point where it was time to decide. He basically said, "Alright, Lord, I have done all of these things. I have sought Your guidance. I have studied Your Word, and now I trust You to sanctify my judgment because I am putting aside my own will and I only want Your will to be done. So I am going to exercise my judgment based upon all of your Spirit, and this is what I have decided."

And did this plan work? Let Mr. Mueller's testimony answer: "I never remember," he wrote three years before his death, "in my entire Christian course, a period now of sixty-nine years and four months that I ever *sincerely* and *patiently* sought to know the will of God by the teaching of the Holy Ghost, through the instrumentality of the Word of God, but I have been always directed rightly. But if honesty of heart and uprightness before God were lacking or if I did not patiently wait upon God for instruction, or if I preferred the counsel of my fellow men to the declarations of the Word of the living God, I made great mistakes."

Inward peace may be indicative of a good conscience, which, if well instructed by Scripture, may be helpful in discerning the will of God. Yet inward peace is not infallible evidence that we are in the right way. Sometimes the will of God leads us into trials that may occasion anxiety. If inward peace were Jesus' criterion for discerning His Father's will, would He ever have gone to the cross? See Matthew 26:38: "My soul is exceeding sorrowful, even unto death."

God and Our Needs

Finally, brethren, from the pen of inspiration we are told, "Our Lord adapts Himself to our special needs. He is a shade on our right hand. He walks close by our side, ready to supply all our necessities. He comes very near to those who are engaged in willing service for Him. He knows everyone by name. O what assurances we have of the tender love of Christ" (White, *SDA Bible Commentary, vol. 3,* p. 1153.8).

"Our heavenly Father has a thousand ways to provide for us of which we know nothing. Those who accept the one principle of making the service of God supreme, will find perplexities vanish, and a plain path before their feet" (White, *The Ministry of Healing*, p. 481).

"If you watch and wait and pray, Providence and revelation will guide you through all the perplexities that you will meet, so that you will not fail nor become discouraged… But Providence is still in our world, working among those who are grasping for the truth. These will recognize the hand of God" (White, *General Conference Bulletin,* June 6, 1913, p. 289.3).

"The supply in our hands may seem to fall far short of our needs; but in the hands of the Lord it will be more than sufficient. The servitor "set it before them, and they did eat, and left thereof, according to the word of the Lord" (White, *Testimonies for the Church,* vol. 6, p. 466.3).

God wants every one of us to come to Him as little children come to their parents. He wants us to ask Him in faith, without doubt, for grace to supply our needs. "If any of you lack wisdom, let him ask of God, that giveth to all men liberally, and upbraideth not; and it shall be given him" (James 1:5).

CHAPTER 6

THE CHRISTIAN ARMOR

The Bible tells us we are in a war, and the devil is bent on destroying us. And we need now, more than ever, weapons of Christian warfare. What is the nature of these weapons? "For the weapons of our warfare *are* not carnal, but mighty through God to the pulling down of strong holds" (2 Cor. 10:4). To be able to withstand the enemy's aggression, God has provided us with some powerful weapons. What are these weapons able to conquer? "Casting down imaginations, and every high thing that exalteth itself against the knowledge of God, and bringing into captivity every thought to the obedience of Christ" (v. 5).

This is a comprehensive defense strategy, and we have to pay attention to it. In this defense strategy, what are we to put on? "Put on the whole armor of God that ye may be able to stand against the wiles of the devil" (Eph. 6:11). If we are to win this combat with the forces of darkness, we need the whole armor. It is not, however, a warfare in which guns and bombs are used; it's a spiritual warfare, where life does not end with physical death, but eternal death, or eternal glory.

The Belt of Truth

What are the first essentials of the needed armor? "Stand therefore, having your loins girt about with truth" (Eph. 6:14). To gird our loins is to fasten the belt of truth around our waists. The word "fasten" indicates the typical use of a belt to support clothing or store tools and weapons. Our lives are supported by the truth of God as it was given to us by the Lord Jesus Christ, whereby we acknowledge, believe, and live by this truth.

The Bible says, "And ye shall know the truth, and the truth shall make you free" (John 8:32). Truth alone can make people free. The belt of truth does not only involve believing the truth but also settling into it, intellectually and spiritually, thus coming to the position where we cannot be moved by the winds of false doctrine.

The Breastplate of Righteousness

What's the breastplate of righteousness (see Eph. 6:14)? The function of the breastplate is to protect our vital organs, especially the heart, from any possible attack from our enemy. There are two kinds of righteousness: justification and sanctification. "Justification means that the conscience, purged from dead works, is placed where it can receive the blessings of sanctification" (White 1957, p. 908).

Sanctification is not merely a theory, emotion, or formality of words, but a living, active principle that infuses one's everyday life. It requires that our habits of eating, drinking, and dressing testify that we are sons and daughters of the heavenly King. This is a daily life of obedience to all God's commandments. When Jesus pardoned the harlot, He said to her, "Go and sin no more."

The Gospel of Peace

With what are the feet of the children of God to be shod? "And your feet shod with the preparation of the gospel of peace" (Eph. 6:15). The last piece of armor Paul mentions in Ephesians 6 is the shoes of the preparation of the gospel of peace. What purpose did shoes serve for a Roman soldier? What purpose do these spiritual shoes serve for us? Imagine a fully-armed soldier. He has his sword, shield, helmet, breastplate, and belt, but his feet are completely bare. The picture probably seems strange, and it should. Just by thinking about it we can tell something is missing.

With that said, the problem goes beyond just looking odd. A shoeless soldier could run into real trouble in the heat of battle. Unless he is fighting on artificial grass, he is going to encounter some debris. It may be nothing more than twigs and pebbles, but to a bare foot that can cause severe pain, and one of the last things you want to deal with in the middle of a fight is worrying about where you step.

In short, shoes allow us to step freely and without fear while we turn our full attention to the battle at hand. My brethren, these are the directions given to us by God. Let no person complicate or mystify the plain directions given by the highest Authority. This is what the Bible says: "How beautiful upon the mountains are the feet of him that bringeth good tidings, that publisheth peace; that bringeth good tidings of good, that publisheth salvation; that saith unto Zion, Thy God reigneth" (Isa. 52:7)!

"The gospel is a message of peace. Christianity is a system, which, received and obeyed, would spread peace, harmony, and happiness throughout the earth. The religion of Christ will unite in close brotherhood all who accepts its teachings.… The only power that can create or perpetuate true peace is the grace of Christ" (White 1973, p. 32). "Let the message of warning be given clear and distinct. The Lord is coming to execute judgment upon all who obey not the gospel" (White 1923, p. 230).

The Shield of Faith

What piece of armor is next mentioned as necessary? "Above all, taking the shield of faith, wherewith ye shall be able to quench all the fiery darts of the wicked" (Eph. 6:16). The shield is the barrier between the body of the soldier and the weapon of the foe. It protects us from the enemy's attempt to seriously or fatally wound us, as indicated by the fiery darts (missile, spear, or arrow). Our faith allows the power of God to extinguish that weapon or attack directed against us.

Faith is an essential part of the Christian life. On the divine ladder of experience by which the Christian rises in triumph over every obstacle, faith is used in connection with prayer and every act and experience of life. Without faith, prayer is a mockery and valueless. "[P]rayer is the key in the hand of faith to unlock heaven's storehouse, where are treasured the boundless resources of Omnipotence" (White 1892, pp. 94, 95).

The Helmet of Salvation

What armor is the Christian to put on as protection for his or her head? "And take the helmet of salvation" (Eph. 6:17). The greatest point of vulnerability for a soldier in combat is his head. He protects his head from injury by wearing a helmet. The head is the seat of our mind and spirit. In 1 Thessalonians 5:8, the helmet is called "the hope of salvation." Therefore, the hope of salvation will preserve courage and aid in protecting the spiritual life of the Christian pilgrim when beset by the enemy of righteousness.

The Sword of the Spirit

What is the sword of the Christian soldier? "[A]nd the sword of the Spirit, which is the word of God" (Eph. 6:17). The sword is a weapon with a long blade for cutting or thrusting that is often used as an instrument of destruction or combat. In modern warfare, soldiers use long-distance weapons. They launch missiles toward targets which they locate by radar and may never see the target they are trying to destroy.

In Paul's day, all battles were fought in close-up, hand-to-hand combat. When the Holy Spirit commanded our use of the sword, He intended that it should be used in personal fighting, face-to-face with the enemy. Therefore, the war is to be fought directly with Satan or his agents. To fight, you have to face the enemy, move close to him, and use your strength to thrust the sword against him. You can only do two things with a sword to hurt an enemy: cut with the edge or thrust with the point.

You can only do two things to defend yourself with a sword: block the enemy's sword when he tries to cut you or knock it aside when he tries to thrust the point at you. In these last days, Satan is raging. Ungodly people are taking counsel together, and we are threatened with war. Now is the time to let people know that we are all exposed to the edge of the sword and rage of the devil. Unless we wake up, we are goners.

The battle is won on our knees. As we pray and fight this spiritual war, we must be clad with the whole armor of God

What is the sword of the spirit? "For the word of God *is* quick, and powerful, and sharper than any twoedged sword, piercing even to the dividing asunder of soul and spirit, and of the joints and marrow, and *is* a discerner of the thoughts and intents of the heart" (Heb. 4:12). Paul, throughout his epistles, speaks of the reality of spiritual warfare and issues particular challenges to us.

"Fight the good fight of faith, lay hold on eternal life, whereunto thou art also called, and hast professed a good profession before many witnesses" (1 Tim. 6:12).

"No man that warreth entangleth himself with the affairs of *this* life; that he may please him who hath chosen him to be a soldier" (2 Tim. 2:4)

"Put on the whole armour of God, that ye may be able to stand against the wiles of the devil. For we wrestle not against flesh and blood, but against principalities, against powers, against the rulers of the darkness of this world, against spiritual wickedness in high *places*" (Eph. 6:11, 12).

The battle is won on our knees. As we pray and fight this spiritual war, we must be clad with the whole armor of God. We must take up the sword and go on the offensive. We must attack Satan at his own stronghold. We must choose the time and place to launch out, and our devotional and prayer time is the ideal time. The *place* of wrestling is also important, and it should be private and apart from others. Deep communion with God is difficult when others are present and busy with other activities.

Triple Remedy

"I counsel thee to buy of me gold tried in the fire, that thou mayest be rich; and white raiment, that thou mayest be clothed, and *that* the shame of thy nakedness do not appear; and anoint thine eyes with eyesalve, that thou mayest see" (Rev. 3:18). The triple affliction of Laodicea—poverty, nakedness, and blindness—is cured with the marvelous triple remedy of heaven:

1. Gold tried in the fire to make rich
2. White raiment to cover shame
3. Eye salve to restore sight

What is symbolized by these three items?

"The gold here recommended as having been tried in the fire is faith and love. It makes the heart rich, for it has been purged until it is pure, and the more it is tested the more brilliant is its luster" (White 1977, p. 725).

"The white raiment is the righteousness of Christ that may be wrought into the character. Purity of heart, purity of motive, will characterize every one who is washing his robe, and making it white in the blood of the Lamb" (White 1957, p. 965).

"[T]he eyesalve is that spiritual discernment which will enable you to see the wiles of Satan and shun them, to detect sin and abhor it, to see truth and obey it" (White 1889, p. 233).

One of the first gifts the Holy Spirit gives lukewarm Christians who seek to be liberated from spiritual stupor is eye salve. One may wonder what eye salve is. It is God's spiritual antidote for spiritual blindness. It imparts to the believer the ability to see things that transcend the five common senses. It is God's divine grace that helps a child of God detect sin and abhor it, see the truth and obey it, and recognize the wiles of Satan and shun them. Another name for eye salve is "discernment of the Holy Spirit."

Any believer who does not have this grace is said to be blind, even spiritually dead. Such a person will always walk into the net of the enemy and may not be able to detect the subtle manipulations of the powers of darkness. Discernment is the inner communication to a believer from the Holy Spirit. It is only those whose lives are subject to the will of God who receive direct communication from the Holy Spirit.

How does the Holy Spirit speak to us? He speaks to us through the Word of God, the Bible, as well as through thoughts. He flashes a thought through one's spirit into one's mind. This is one reason why it is so important to scrutinize our thoughts and ask the Lord to keep our minds and hearts pure. The Holy Spirit sometimes injects a burden and directs us to some form of action, such as prayer, which is productive. He speaks to us through dreams, revelations, and even circumstances. We need to be in the Spirit all the time.

CHAPTER 7

PREVAILING PRAYER

Prayer is a solemn and humble supplication, with an expression of thanks and praises to God Almighty. In prayer we open our hearts to God, talking to Him as a loving Father and Friend. Prayer brings us closer to Him. How willing is He to hear and answer our prayers? "If ye then, being evil, know how to give good gifts unto your children, how much more shall your Father which is in heaven give good things to them that ask him" (Matthew 7:11)?

"Every good gift and every perfect gift is from above, and cometh down from the Father of lights, with whom is no variableness, neither shadow of turning" (James 1:17). Prayer is the key in the hand of faith to unlock heaven's storehouse, where there are treasured and boundless resources of omnipotence. How shall we pray, that we may be heard and receive help from God? "Praying always with all prayer and supplication in the Spirit" (Eph. 6:18).

Praying in the Spirit

If God is to hear us and grant our requests, we must always pray in the Spirit. Why must we pray in the Spirit? "God *is* a Spirit: and they that worship him must worship *him* in spirit and in truth" (John 4:24). Because God is a spirit, whatever we do that involves Him must be done in the Spirit. How do we pray and worship in the Spirit? If we are to understand how to pray and worship God in the Spirit, we must go to the Holy Scriptures and see how the apostles prayed to and worshiped God.

It may appear confusing to some of those who are seeking to understand the context of the word "spirit," whether the Bible is referring to a person's spirit or God/the Holy Spirit. That brings us to this question: "With which spirit are we to pray and worship God? "For God is my witness, whom I serve with my spirit in the gospel of his Son that without ceasing I make mention of you always in my prayers" (Rom. 1:9).

The apostle Paul spoke of serving God with his spirit, even in praying and interceding for others. The above text shows the involvement of mankind's spirit in the act of worship and service to God. How does God's Spirit respond to a person's spirit? "The Spirit itself beareth witness with our spirit, that we are the children of God" (Rom. 8:16).

Keep in mind that God's Spirit cannot bear witness with one's spirit unless the two are fused together. In other words, Paul is trying to tell us that the Spirit of God must be connected with a person's spirit to confirm him or her as His child. That's why he commented, "For as many as are led by the Spirit of God, they are the sons of God" (v. 14).

With this understanding, we can now answer the question regarding how we should pray to be heard and helped by God. First of all, we have to note that God's Spirit must fuse with our spirit and direct us as we pray in Him. What condition describes one who is in the Spirit? "The LORD *is* nigh unto them that are of a broken heart; and saveth such as be of a contrite spirit". (Ps. 34:18). "The sacrifices of God *are* a broken spirit: a broken and a contrite heart, O God, thou wilt not despise" (51:17). "He healeth the broken in heart, and bindeth up their wounds" (147:3).

Broken heart/contrite spirit is the condition of the heart touched by the Holy Spirit. What is a broken heart? A broken heart is defined as "feeling great sorrow; completely miserable and helpless; overwhelmed by grief or disappointment," while a contrite spirit means "feeling or expressing remorse." Until we have real desire in our hearts and sense a desperate need for what we are asking God, realizing our total dependence only on Him, our prayers of little to no meaning, because formality of words does not make a prayer, but an intense , longing desire for and absolute dependence on God are what really move Him. What does the Spirit of God do with our prayers?

The Pleading of the Spirit

"Likewise the Spirit also helpeth our infirmities: for we know not what we should pray for as we ought: but the Spirit itself maketh intercession for us with groanings which cannot be uttered. And he that searcheth the hearts knoweth what *is* the mind of the Spirit, because he maketh intercession for the saints according to *the will of* God" (Rom. 8:26, 27).

Here we are told that God's Spirit takes up our prayer requests and present them before God in a restructured manner. He already knows the will of the Father, and by directing our spirits, He understands every bit of our hearts' desires, so He takes up our requests and presents them before God according to His will. What happens when we ask according to God's will? "And this is the confidence that we have in him, that, if we ask any thing according to his will, he heareth us: And if we know that he hear us, whatsoever we ask, we know that we have the petitions that we desired of him" (1 John 5:14, 15).

God hears us whenever we ask anything according to His will. And we cannot ask according to His will if we do not pray in the Spirit. It is only when we pray in the Spirit that we can perfectly ask according to His will, for the Bible says:

> But God hath revealed *them* unto us by his Spirit: for the Spirit searcheth all things, yea, the deep things of God. For what man knoweth the things of a man, save the spirit of man which is in him? even so the things of God knoweth no man, but the Spirit of God. Now we have received, not the spirit of the world, but the spirit which is of God; that we might know the things that are freely given to us of God. (1 Corinthians 2:10–12)

Do you see how perfectly the Word of God has established the truth? To have effective communication with God, we need the Holy Spirit. In other words, God's Spirit must always direct our spirits.

The Life of Praying

"And it came to pass, when Moses held up his hand, that Israel prevailed: and when he let down his hand, Amalek prevailed" (Ex. 17:11). As the children of Israel were returning from Egypt, after crossing the Red Sea and heading to Sinai, they encounter the Amalekites, a fierce, warlike tribe that inhabited that region. They came out after the children of Israel for war. Then Moses directed Joshua to lead a body of soldiers to confront these wicked foes, while he went on the top of the mountain to pray.

> *It is interesting to note that it wasn't Moses' choice to lower his hands; he was weary. However, the enemies never cared if it was weariness or not; all they wanted was victory, and they were prevailing. Therefore, Moses asked Aaron and Hur to help him hold his hands up so Joshua and Israel could win*

As the battle raged between Israel and the Amalekites, Moses was on the top of the mountain with the rod of God in his hand outstretched towards heaven. When he raised his hand higher, Joshua, who was on the bottom of the mountain, would be winning, but when his hands got tired and lowered, Joshua began to lose.

It is interesting to note that it wasn't Moses' choice to lower his hands; he was weary. However, the enemies never cared if it was weariness or not; all they wanted was victory, and they were prevailing. Therefore, Moses asked Aaron and Hur to help him hold his hands up so Joshua and Israel could win.

Dear friends, this picture describes our lives, which have two parts: Moses on top of the mountain and Joshua on the bottom of the mountain. The things we do in our prayer closet at the top decides how successful we are going to be in our daily lives below. To be successful both in our physical and spiritual lives, we must make prayer a habit and do so in the spirit.

Israel's Experience

And it came to pass in process of time that the king of Egypt died: and the children of Israel sighed by reason of the bondage, and they cried, and their cry came up unto God by reason of the bondage. And God heard their groaning, and God remembered his covenant with Abraham, with Isaac, and with Jacob. And God looked upon the children of Israel, and God had respect unto *them*. (Ex. 2:23–25)

What Is Sighing?

To sigh means to take a long, deep breath that can be heard, which typically reflects an experience of sadness, relief, or tiredness. The children of Israel sighed under the heavy hands of the Egyptian bondage. The Holy Spirit, the author of the Holy Scriptures, found it necessary to leave us a record that Jesus, while looking up to heaven "sighed" (see Mark 7:34). Sighing is a form of communication. It denotes intensity, burden, release, emotion, and expression that cannot be translated to another language; it transcends all languages. By sighing, Jesus communicated to the Father without a word, and the Father understood Him. Jesus had four ways of expressing His needs in prayer: spiritually, emotionally, mentally, and physically.

Describing the events of the last days, Ezekiel 9:2–6 highlights those who will specially receive the seal of God among the final generation of believers. The sealing angel, with the writer's inkhorn, placed God's seal on those who were seen sighing and crying for the sins committed on the earth and in the midst of His people. Sighing is indeed a form of communication.

What else were the children of Israel seen doing at the same time they were sighing? "And God heard their groaning, and God remembered his covenant with Abraham, with Isaac, and with Jacob. And God looked upon the children of Israel, and God had respect unto *them*" (Ex. 2:24, 25).

What Is Groaning?

A groan is a deep, sad, inarticulate sound conveying pain, despair, or sometimes pleasure. One who groans makes a low creaking sound when pressure or weight is applied, or when beneath or under oppression. We are told that the Israelites' groaning caught God's attention, and that He remembered His covenant with Abraham. Please note that these people were the fourth generation of the descendants of Abraham, who had not yet witnessed the mighty dealings of God.

All through their lives, they had been living in Egypt. As a matter of fact, they were all born in Egypt. They knew not any other worship style except the ones they constantly observed among the Egyptians. Therefore, they had no legitimate conception of how the worship of the only true Jehovah God looked.

That was why at that darkest moment of their lives, it never occurred to them to pray or channel their cries to God. However, the heart of our merciful and compassionate Father was bending low towards them. Their groaning, like a thick cloud of smoke, ascended before the throne of God as a supplication. Our groaning can speak for us; our groaning is also a prayer. God, because of His love, finds it irresistible.

So far in our study on the subject of prayer, we've come to understand what constitutes the spirit of humanity and what is meant by praying in the Spirit. Let's move on to the next component of this subject.

Watching unto Prayer

Unto what are we exhorted to watch? "But the end of all things is at hand: be ye therefore sober, and watch unto prayer" (1 Peter 4:7). How general is the command to watch? "And what I say unto you I say unto all, Watch" (Mark 13:37).

What does it mean to watch unto prayer? Jesus used this phrase on a couple of different occasions. The word translated "watch" means "to have the alertness of a guard at night." A night watchperson must be even more vigilant than a daytime guard. In the daytime, danger can often be spotted from a distance.

However, during the night, everything is different. A night guard must use senses other than sight to detect danger. He is often alone in the darkness, and without the defenses, he would otherwise employ. There may be no indications of an enemy attack until it happens, so he must be hypervigilant, suspecting something at any moment. That is the type of watching about which Jesus spoke.

What is one of the petitions of the Lord's Prayer? "Lead us not into temptation, but deliver us from evil (Matt. 6:13). By what means can we escape temptation? "Watch and pray, that ye enter not into temptation" (26:41). To overcome temptation, we must be watchful and prayerful. How faithful should we be in this matter? "Praying always with all prayer and supplication in the Spirit, and watching thereunto with all perseverance and supplication for all saints" (Eph. 6:18).

Drowsiness

Many people are aware that there is a spiritual warfare, but only a few know the strategy of the enemy. Do you know that the sleeping state is a time in which the forces of darkness intensify their battle against us? It is well known in occultism and witchcraft operations that no esoteric or metaphysical power can dominate a person who is physically awake unless he or she is at the lowest ebb of spirituality.

Apart from such a state of sinfulness, all the known, projected attacks against a person happen only in a sleepy state. The Bible says, "Watch and pray, that ye enter not into temptation: the spirit indeed *is* willing, but the flesh *is* weak" (Matt. 26:41). I am not saying you should be awake all through the night to consciously fight the forces of darkness. There is time for everything, including getting adequate rest and sleep, as well as prayer. We are expected to go to bed early so we can wake up early in the morning to pray.

It is during the darkest hours in our sleep state, between 2:00 a.m. and 4:00 a.m., when the forces of darkness intensify their battle against us. "But while men slept, his enemy came and sowed tares among the wheat, and went his way" (Matt. 13:25). The Bible further says, "Give not sleep to thine eyes, nor slumber to thine eyelids. Deliver thyself as a roe from the hand *of the hunter*, and as a bird from the hand of the fowler" (Prov. 6:4, 5).

Jesus said, "Watch and pray." Why? So that we do not enter into temptation. What if we do not watch and pray? The answer is we will enter into temptation. Note that our Lord did not say, "Watch *or* pray." He said,

"Watch *and* pray." Therefore, we cannot do one and leave out the other; we must do both simultaneously. It is only then that we can overcome the manipulations of the prince of darkness.

No believer can effectively watch without the grace and discernment of the Spirit. That brings us to this important question: What is the discernment of the Spirit?

Discernment of the Spirit

Spiritual discernment is an endowment of the Holy Spirit given to a believer to enable him or her to distinguish between good and evil, holy and unholy, and truth and error, whether it be in an encounter, event, or prophetic message. One of the benefits of having a gift of discernment is a heightened awareness of God's presence. However, not only can we discern what the Spirit of God is doing, but also the snares of the enemy. Spiritual discernment makes the believer more sensitive to the spiritual atmosphere around him or her.

In the early developing stages, believers may be adversely affected by the presence of demonic activity in the environment around them. The reality is that we concurrently live in a natural world and spiritual world. In the Bible, when Jacob came across a group of angels, he named that place "Mahanaim," meaning "double camp" (see Gen. 32:1, 2). As Jacob realized, we also live in a double camp where there is constant spiritual activity, and discerners have spiritual senses that are attuned to this.

The ability to know what lies behind a person's words or actions is another benefit of the gift of discernment. It helps the believer know whether someone is telling the truth or not. Regarding a prophetic or revelatory message, a discerner can often tell whether it is of the Lord or not.

Hearing God Speak

Prayer is communication between God and us. If you've never heard God speak to you, then you have a wonderful experience awaiting you as you grow in prayer. More than anything, God wants to communicate with us. What are the various ways in which God, through the Holy Spirit, communicates with believers?

1. The Bible and Spirit of Prophecy
2. Impressions of the Holy Spirit in the heart
3. Dream-like revelations
4. Spiritually sharpened intuition
5. His creation

The Holy Spirit not only delights to give inner suggestions, but also shows us what not to do, say, or even pray. He restrained Paul in his prayer (see 2 Cor. 12:7–9). If you train yourself to listen and be sensitive to the Holy Spirit, you will find His restraining very real and frequent. Have you ever wondered how Jesus knew exactly where to go and what to do on a particular day? The discerning and the guidance ministry of the Holy Spirit is an important aspect of God's providential government of the universe. It is part of the manifestation of His grace to mankind.

Three Prayer Modes

It is impossible for the soul to flourish when prayer is not a special exercise of the mind. Jesus taught His disciples that only the prayer which arises from unfeigned lips and is genuine and prompted by the actual wants of the soul would bring heaven's blessings to the petitioner. There are three prayer circles: public, family, and private (or secret).

"Family or public prayer alone is not sufficient. Secret prayer is very important; in solitude the soul is laid bare to the inspecting eye of God, and every motive is scrutinized" (White 2002, p. 178).

> Private prayer, family prayer, prayer in public gatherings for the worship of God—all is essential. And we are to live our prayers. We are to co-operate with Christ in His work....
>
> ...If ever there was a time when every house should be a house of prayer it is now....
>
> ...Prayer, whether offered in the public assembly, at the family altar, or in secret, places man directly in the presence of God. By constant prayer the youth may obtain principles so firm that the most powerful temptations will not draw them from their allegiance to God....
>
> ...We should pray to God much more than we do. There is great strength and blessing in praying together in our families, with and for our children. When my children have done wrong, and I have talked with them kindly and then prayed with them, I have never found it necessary after that to punish them. Their hearts would melt in tenderness before the Holy Spirit that came in answer to prayer....
>
> ...High-flown language is inappropriate in prayer, whether the petition be offered in the pulpit, in the family circle, or in secret. Especially should the one offering public prayer use simple language that others may understand what is said and unite with the petition.
>
> It is the heart-felt prayer of faith that is heard in heaven and answered on earth....

…Your children should be educated to be kind, thoughtful of others, gentle, easy to be entreated, and, above everything else, to respect religious things and feel the importance of the claims of God. They should be taught to respect the hour of prayer; they should be required to rise in the morning so as to be present at family worship.…

…We should not come to the house of God to pray for our families unless deep feeling shall lead us while the Spirit of God is convicting them. Generally, the proper place to pray for our families is at the family altar. When the subjects of our prayers are at a distance, the closet is the proper place to plead with God for them. When in the house of God, we should pray for a present blessing and should expect God to hear and answer our prayers. Such meetings will be lively and interesting.…

…In many cases the morning and evening worship is little more than a mere form, a dull, monotonous repetition of set phrases in which the spirit of gratitude or the sense of need finds no expression. The Lord accepts not such service. But the petitions of a humble heart and contrite spirit He will not despise. The opening of our hearts to our heavenly Father, the acknowledgment of our entire dependence, the expression of our wants, the homage of grateful love—this is true prayer. (White, *Prayer*, pp. 192, 193)

"Cultivate the habit of talking with the Saviour when you are alone, when you are walking, and when you are busy with your daily labor. Let the heart be continually uplifted in silent petition for help, for light, for strength, for knowledge. Let every breath be a prayer" (White 2002, p. 179).

Times of Prayer

Jesus loved to pray. He understood the importance of prayer as communion with His heavenly Father. Certain portions of Scripture speak of the times Jesus found best for His prayer life. How often did He pray? "Evening, and morning, and at noon, will I pray, and cry aloud: and he shall hear my voice" (Ps. 55:17).

1. **Morning**: "And in the morning, rising up a great while before day, he went out, and departed into a solitary place, and there prayed" (Mark 1:35).
2. **Evening**: "And when he had sent the multitudes away, he went up into a mountain apart to pray: and when the evening was come, he was there alone" (Matt. 14:23).

3. **All night**: "And it came to pass in those days, that he went out into a mountain to pray, and continued all night in prayer to God" (Luke 6:12).
4. **Continually**: "Watch ye therefore, and pray always, that ye may be accounted worthy to escape all these things that shall come to pass, and to stand before the Son of man" (Luke 21:36).

These few verses indicate that Jesus Christ lived in unbroken fellowship with His Father through prayer. To Jesus, the places of prayer were meaningful, and these included a mountain, garden, boat, and secret chamber. We are admonished to pray in our closet, and as we go about our daily labor, our hearts are to be often uplifted to God.

Hindrances to Prayer

Do you sometimes feel as if your prayers are not being heard or answered? Often, God delays His answers so that we will seek Him and learn how to be patient. However, we must be aware of the following factors that can make our prayers ineffective and make sure that they do not creep into our lives.

Why is it that our prayers are sometimes not answered? What could be the cause? To be effective, our prayers must be offered according to divine order. The Bible says, "Ask, and it shall be given you; seek, and ye shall find; knock, and it shall be opened unto you" (Matt. 7:7). In this text, we find three key elements: simple words of asking, a settled attitude of seeking, and vigorous, sustained knocking.

1. **Selfishness**: Ask for things in God's will, in that the outcome will honor and glorify Him. When we pray to feed our lusts, God cannot answer our prayers. The Bible says, "Ye lust, and have not: ye kill, and desire to have, and cannot obtain: ye fight and war, yet ye have not, because ye ask not. Ye ask, and receive not, because ye ask amiss, that ye may consume *it* upon your lusts" (James 4:2, 3).

2. **Lack of love for God**: If we don't love God, our prayers will not be answered. How can we seek and find? "I love them that love me; and those that seek me early shall find me" (Prov. 8:17). "And ye shall seek me, and find *me*, when ye shall search for me with all your heart" (Jer. 29:13).

3. **Robbing God in tithes and offerings**: Generosity is the way we knock and open the windows of heaven. The Bible says, "Bring ye all the tithes into the storehouse, that there may be meat in mine house, and prove me now herewith, saith the LORD of hosts, if I will not open you the windows of heaven, and pour you out a blessing, that *there shall* not *be room* enough *to receive it*" (Mal. 3:10).

4. **Doubt and unbelief**: The Bible says, "But let him ask in faith, nothing wavering. For he that wavereth is like a wave of the sea driven with the wind and tossed. For let not that man thinks that he shall receive any thing of the Lord" (James 1:6–7). When we pray with a wavering faith and carry doubt and unbelief, our prayers will not be answered. Doubt is a feeling of uncertainty or lack of conviction. The Bible says, "But without faith *it is* impossible to please *him*: for he that cometh to God must believe that he is, and *that* he is a rewarder of them that diligently seek him" (Heb. 11:6).

5. **Unforgiveness**: "But if ye forgive not men their trespasses, neither will your Father forgive your trespasses" (Matt. 6:15).

6. **Lack of reconciliation**: Bearing malice, hate, or a grudge against anyone can hinder our prayers. The Bible says, "Therefore if thou bring thy gift to the altar, and there rememberest that thy brother hath ought against thee; Leave there thy gift before the altar, and go thy way; first be reconciled to thy brother, and then come and offer thy gift" (Matt. 5:23, 24).

7. **Disharmony in the family or with others**: "Likewise, ye husbands, dwell with *them* according to knowledge, giving honour unto the wife, as unto the weaker vessel, and as being heirs together of the grace of life; that your prayers be not hindered" (1 Peter 3:7).

8. **Failure to ask God to supply our needs**: "yet ye have not, because ye ask not" (James 4:2). If we fail to tell God our needs, they will not be supplied. "Everyone needs a practical experience in trusting God for himself. Let no man become your confessor; open the heart to God; tell Him every secret of the soul. Bring to Him your difficulties, small and great, and He will show you a way

out of them all. He alone can know how to give the very help you need" (White 1915, p. 418).

9. **Neglecting the poor**: "Whoso stoppeth his ears at the cry of the poor, he also shall cry himself, but shall not be heard" (Prov. 21:13). Whenever we turn a deaf ear to those in need, God will not hear our prayers.

Pray back God's words to Him: "Let my supplication come before thee: deliver me according to thy word" (Psalms 119:170).

"Plead my cause, and deliver me: quicken me according to thy word" (v. 154).

"I entreated thy favour with *my* whole heart: be merciful unto me according to thy word" (v. 58).

"Therefore say unto them, Thus saith the Lord GOD; There shall none of my words be prolonged any more, but the word which I have spoken shall be done, saith the Lord GOD" (Ezek. 12:28).

Always search in God's Word and look for that particular verse that speaks about your condition. Claim the promises and rest in God's assurance in faith.

1. **Abiding in Christ**: "If ye abide in me, and my words abide in you, ye shall ask what ye will, and it shall be done unto you" (John 15:7). We have to abide in Christ to always receive from Him.
2. **Disobedience to God's law**: "He that turneth away his ear from hearing the law, even his prayer *shall be* abomination" (Prov. 28:9).
3. Unconfessed sins: "If I regard iniquity in my heart, the Lord will not hear *me*" (Ps. 66:18).
4. Asking according to God's will: "And this is the confidence that we have in him, that, if we ask any thing according to his will, he heareth us" (1 John 5:14).
5. Praying through Jesus: "Ye have not chosen me, but I have chosen you, and ordained you, that ye should go and bring forth fruit, and *that* your fruit should remain: that whatsoever ye shall ask of the Father in my name, he may give it you" (John 15:16).

Kneeling, a Duty or a Choice

- Both in public and in private worship it is our privilege to bow on our knees before God when we offer our petitions to Him. Jesus, our example, **"kneeled down, and prayed."** Luke 22:41. Of His disciples it is recorded that they, too, **"kneeled down, and prayed."** Acts 9:40. Paul declared, **"I bow my knees unto the Father of our**

Lord Jesus Christ." Ephesians 3:14. In confessing before God the sins of Israel, Ezra knelt. See Ezra 9:5. **Daniel "kneeled upon his knees three times a day, and prayed, and gave thanks before his God." Daniel 6:10.** (White, *Prayer*, p. 187)

- **And when thou prayest, thou shalt not be as the hypocrites** *are***: for they love to pray standing in the synagogues and in the corners of the streets, that they may be seen of men. Verily I say unto you, They have their reward.** (Matthew 6:5)
- I have received letters questioning me in regard to the proper attitude to be taken by a person offering prayer to the Sovereign of the universe. Where have our brethren obtained the idea that they should stand upon their feet when praying to God? (White, *The SDA Bible Commentary*, vol. 3, p. 1130)
- **For it is written,** *As* **I live, saith the Lord, every knee shall bow to me, and every tongue shall confess to God.** (Romans 14:11)
- To bow down when in prayer to God is the proper attitude to occupy. This act of worship was required of the three Hebrew captives in Babylon.... But such an act was homage to be rendered to God alone—the Sovereign of the world, the Ruler of the universe; and these three Hebrews refused to give such honor to any idol even though composed of pure gold. In doing so, they would, to all intents and purposes, be bowing to the king of Babylon. Refusing to do as the king had commanded, they suffered the penalty, and were cast into the burning fiery furnace. But Christ came in person and walked with them through the fire, and they received no harm. (White, *Prayer*, pp. 207, 208)
- **That at the name of Jesus every knee should bow, of** *things* **in heaven, and** *things* **in earth, and** *things* **under the earth.** (Philippians 2:10)
- And when you assemble to worship God, be sure and bow your knees before Him. Let this act testify that the whole soul, body, and spirit are in subjection to the Spirit of truth....
- ...True reverence for God is inspired by a sense of His infinite greatness and a realization of His presence. With this sense of the Unseen, every heart should be deeply impressed. The hour and place of prayer are sacred, because God is there; and as reverence is manifested in attitude and demeanor, the feeling that inspires it will be deepened. (White, *Prayer*, pp. 208–210)
- **But what saith the answer of God unto him? I have reserved to myself seven thousand men, who have not bowed the knee to** *the image of* **Baal.** (Romans 11:4)

Biblical Examples

1. Jesus— "And he was **withdrawn from them about a stone's cast, and kneeled down, and prayed**" (Luke 22:41).
2. Paul— "**And when he had thus spoken, he kneeled down, and prayed with them all**" (Acts 20:36).
3. Peter— "**But Peter put them all forth, and kneeled down, and prayed; and turning** *him* **to the body said, Tabitha, arise. And she opened her eyes: and when she saw Peter, she sat up**" (9:40).
4. Stephen— "**And they stoned Stephen, calling upon** *God*, **and saying, Lord Jesus, receive my spirit. And he kneeled down, and cried with a loud voice, Lord, lay not this sin to their charge. And when he had said this, he fell asleep**" (7:59, 60).
5. Apostles— "**And when we had accomplished those days, we departed and went our way; and they all brought us on our way, with wives and children, till** *we were* **out of the city: and we kneeled down on the shore, and prayed**" (21:5).
6. Ezra— "And **at the evening sacrifice I arose up from my heaviness; and having rent my garment and my mantle, I fell upon my knees, and spread out my hands unto the LORD my God**" (Ezra 9:5).
7. Psalmist— "**O come, let us worship and bow down: let us kneel before the LORD our maker**" (Ps. 95:6).

And this whole chapter will, if the heart is receptive, be as precious a lesson as we can learn. Therefore, friends, to bow down when in prayer to God is the proper position.

King Solomon stood upon a brazen scaffold before the altar, and blessed the people. He then knelt down, and, with his hands raised upward, poured forth earnest and solemn prayer to God, while the congregations were bowed with their faces to the ground. After Solomon had ended his prayer, a miraculous fire came from Heaven and consumed the sacrifice. (White, *The Spirit of Prophecy*, vol. 1, p. 414)

CHAPTER 8

BATTLE IN THE REALM OF PRAYER

Beloved, I find it opportune, in these times when the forces of darkness are on a rampage, battling the children of God, to put at your disposal a testimony of a former Satanist, narrated by Pastor John Mulinde as well as the vision of a Christian lady. In fact, the bulk of this chapter is adapted from both the testimony of this former Satanist and a nineteenth-century, Christian author, Ellen G. White, although supplemented with my own remarks.

This testimony reveals to us how the devil does everything to prevent us from waging a victorious spiritual war. While the vision of this Christian woman seems to confirm that every child of God has an enemy to overcome, John began his testimony by telling the story of how someone who had served the devil for a long time finally gave his life to Christ. After his conversion, he gave his testimony:

> This man was born after his parents dedicated themselves to Lucifer. When he was still in the womb, they performed so many rituals dedicating him to serve Lucifer. When he was four years old, he began to exercise his spiritual power. And his parents began fearing him. When he was six years, his father brought him to some witches for them to train him. And by the time he was ten years old, he was doing tremendous exploits for the kingdom of the devil. He was feared by the common witches. (http://1ref.us/rm, [accessed 2/27,2019])

The idea that a person can be possessed by evil spirits against their will is as old as man. Although medical science in general remains skeptical, some psychiatrists believes demonic possession is indeed very real. The

Bible recorded this: **"And the people with one accord gave heed unto those things which Philip spake, hearing and seeing the miracles which he did. For unclean spirits, crying with loud voice came out of many that were possessed [with them]: and many taken with palsies, and that were lame, were healed"** (Acts 8:6–7).

In returning to Pastor John's testimony of this boy we read:

> He was still a young boy, but he was so terrible in the things he did. He grew up to be a young man in his twenties with a lot of blood on his hands. He killed at will. He had the ability to leave his body through transcendental meditation. And could levitate; at times his body would rise off the ground and hang in the midair. Sometimes he would go into a trance and leave his body; his body would remain behind, while he went out into the world, by a practice called astral-travelling. And this guy was used by Satan to destroy or divide many churches, and to ruin many pastors. (http://1ref.us/rm, [accessed 2/27/2019])

> From the pen of inspiration we read, "I have been shown that evil angels in the form of believers will work in our ranks to bring in a strong spirit of unbelief. Let not even these discourage you, but bring a true heart to the help of the Lord against the powers of satanic agencies. (White, *Selected Messages*, Vol. 3. p. 410.2)

> These powers of evil will assemble in our meetings, not to receive a blessing, but to counterwork the influences of the Spirit of God. Take up no remark that they may make, but repeat the rich promises of God, which are yea and amen in Christ Jesus". (White, Selected Messages, Vol. 3. p. 410.3)

Dear brethren, if we must overcome these ruthless and wicked forces of darkness that never tires nor sleeps, we must keep the armor on; we must find strength in Christ to overcome them otherwise we'll be overcome by them and lose our souls. The Bible admonishes, **"Be sober, be vigilant; because your adversary the devil, as a roaring lion, walketh about, seeking whom he may devour"** (1 Peter 5:8).

In this story of this devil-possessed young man we are told how,

> He led expeditions through the air. He would go with other satanic agents and many demon spirits. It was as if they were working a shift, in the same way that you've got to go and work your shift. He had a regular time that he was required to go and wage war in the heavenlies. He said that in the heavenlies, in the spiritual realm, if the land is covered by a blanket of darkness, the blanket is so dense it is like solid

rock. And it covers the whole area. The spirits are able to go on top and below the blanket, and from there influence the events on earth.

When the evil spirits and human satanic agents finish their shifts they go down on earth at the points of covenant, on waters or on the land, to refresh their spirit. How do they refresh their spirit? By the sacrifices that people give at these altars. They could be sacrifices in open witchcraft, sacrifices in bloodshed of all types, including abortion, warfare, human and animal sacrifices. They could be sacrifices of sexual immorality, in which people practice sexual perversions and all kinds of promiscuity. And that act services the strength of these powers. There are many different types of sacrifices. (http://1ref.us/rm, [accessed 2/27/2019])

From the pen of inspiration we read, "The adversary seeks continually to obstruct the way to the mercy-seat, that we may not by earnest supplication and faith obtain grace and power to resist temptation" (White, *Steps to Christ*, p. 95). Also, "Our great adversary is constantly seeking to keep the troubled soul away from God. An appeal to Heaven by the humblest saint is more to be dreaded by Satan than the decrees of cabinets or the mandates of kings" (White, *In Heavenly Places*, p. 82).

Do not think that Satan is not doing anything. Do not think that his army is passive. He and his agencies are on the ground today. We are to put on the whole armor of God. Having done all, we are to stand, meeting principalities and powers and spiritual wickedness in high places. And if we have on the heavenly armor, we shall find that the assaults of the enemy will not have power over us. Angels of God will be round about us to protect us. I have the assurance of God that thus it will be. (White, *Ye Shall Receive Power*, p. 239.4)

EVERY PRAYER SMOKES

Pastor John, in discussing this possessed man, also talked about lots of things which really troubled my mind. He said that when they are up there and the Christians begin to pray on earth, the prayers of the Christians appear to them in three forms:

All prayers appear like smoke that is rising up into the heaven. Some prayers appear like smoke that drifts along and vanish in the air. These prayers come from people who have sin in their lives that they are not willing to deal with it. Their prayers are so weak; they are blown and they disappear in the air.

Another type of prayer is also like smoke. It rises upward until it reaches the rock; it cannot break through the rock. These prayers usually come from people who try to purify themselves, but who lack faith as they pray. They usually ignore the other important aspects that are needed when someone prays.

The third type of prayer is like smoke that is filled with fire. As it rises upward, it is so hot that when it reaches the rock, the rock begins to melt like wax. It pierces the rock and goes through

Many times, as people begin to pray, their prayers look like the first type. But as they continue praying, their prayers change and become like the second type of prayer. And as they continue praying, suddenly their prayer ignites into flames. Their prayers become so powerful that they pierce through the rock. (http://1ref.us/rm, [accessed 2/27/2019])

What makes our prayers to appear like fire? **"And the smoke of the incense, [which came] with the prayers of the saints, ascended up before God out of the angel's hand, and the angel took the censer, and filled it with fire of the altar"** (Rev. 8:4–5).

From the pen of inspiration, we are told that it is the glowing fire of Christ's righteousness:

> The religious services, the prayers, the praise, the penitent confession of sin ascend from true believers as incense to the heavenly sanctuary, but passing through the corrupt channels of humanity, they are so defiled that unless purified by blood, they can never be of value with God. They ascend not in spotless purity, and unless the Intercessor, who is at God's right hand, presents and purifies all by His righteousness, it is not acceptable to God ... Oh, that all may see that everything in obedience, in penitence, in praise and thanksgiving, **must be placed upon the glowing fire of the righteousness of Christ. The fragrance of this righteousness ascends like a cloud around the mercy seat**. (White, *Selected Messages*, vol. 1, p. 344.3)

Between the cherubim was a golden censer, and as the prayers of the saints, offered in faith, came up to Jesus, and He presented them to His Father, a cloud of fragrance arose from the incense, looking like smoke of most beautiful colors. Above the place where Jesus stood, before the ark, was exceedingly **bright glory** that I could not look upon; it appeared like the throne of God. As the incense ascended to the Father, the excellent glory came from the throne to Jesus, and from Him it was shed upon those whose prayers had come up like sweet incense. **Light poured upon Jesus in rich abundance and overshadowed the mercy seat, and the train of glory filled the temple. I could not long look upon the surpassing brightness. No language can describe it. I was overwhelmed and turned from the majesty and glory of the scene.** (White, *Early Writings*, p. 252)

When our prayer passes through the purifying process of the precious *blood* of Christ, His merit of righteousness *purifies our prayer.* It then ascends in spotless purity, covered by the fire of His righteousness. A light of glory from Christ overshadows the mercy seat and takes up our matter with a groaning which cannot be altered. The kingdom of darkness trembles. In the Spirit of Prophecy we read:

> If our eyes could be opened to see the good and evil agencies at work, there would be no trifling, no vanity, no jesting or joking. If all would put on the whole armor of God and fight manfully the battles of the Lord, victories would be gained that would cause the kingdom of darkness to tremble. (White, *Testimonies for the Church,* vol. 6, p. 41.1)

What further things are we told from the confession Pastor John shares that happen to us when our prayers become acceptable before the Father?

> Many times evil agents would notice the prayers were changing and coming very close to becoming fire. These agents would then communicate with other spirits on earth and tell them, "Distract that person from prayer. Stop them from praying. Pull them out." And many times Christians yield to these distractions. They are pressing through, repenting and allowing the Word to check their spirit. Their Faith is growing. Their prayers are becoming more focused. (http://1ref.us/rm, [accessed 2/27/2019])

SATAN REJOICES WHEN PRAYERS ARE SPOKEN INDISTINCTLY: Let those who pray and those who speak pronounce their words properly and speak in clear, distinct, even tones. Prayer, if properly offered, is a power for good. It is one of the means used by the Lord to communicate to the people the precious treasures of truth. But prayer is not what it should be, because of the defective voices of those who utter it. Satan rejoices when the prayers offered to God are almost inaudible. Let God's people learn how to speak and pray in a way that will properly represent the great truths they possess. Let the testimonies borne and the prayers offered be clear and distinct. Thus God will be glorified. (White, *Testimonies for the Church,* vol. 6, p. 382)

As the prayer of the saint becomes focused and properly offered,

Then the devil notices that their prayers are gaining strength, and the distractions begin. Telephones ring. Sometimes in the middle of very, very intense prayer, the telephone rings and you think you can go to answer it and then come back and continue praying. However when you return, you go back to the beginning. And that's what the devil wants. Other kinds of distractions come your way. They may touch your body, bringing pain somewhere. They may make you hungry, and you want to go to the kitchen to prepare something to eat. As long as they can get you out of that place, they have defeated you.

If the people persist in this kind of prayer and allow themselves to be inspired in the spirit and to keep going, something happens in the spirit. The fire touches that rock, and it melts. [When the] melting begins, it is so hot that no demon spirit can stand it. No human spirit can stand it. They all flee. They run away.

There comes an opening in the spiritual realm. As soon as it appears, all this trouble in prayer stops. The person who is praying on the ground feels like their prayer has suddenly become so smooth, so enjoyable, so powerful and intense. I've discovered at that moment, we normally lose all awareness of time and other things. Not that we become disorderly. God takes care of our time. But it is as if you lay down everything, and you hook up with God … from that moment on there is no resistance at all, and the person praying can continue as long as he wants. There is no resistance to stop him.

Then he said, after the person finishes praying, the hole remains open. He said that when people rise from their place of prayer, and move on, the open hole moves along with them. They are no longer operating under the blanket. They are operating under an open heaven. He said in that state, the devil cannot do what he wants against them. The presence of the Lord is like a pillar from heaven resting on their lives.

They are protected, and there is so much power inside the pillar that as they move around, the presence touches other people as well. It discerns what the enemy has done in other people. And as they talk to people who are standing with them, they too come inside this pillar. And as long as they stay inside that pillar, all the bondages placed on them by the enemy weaken. (http://1ref.us/rm, [accessed 2/27/2019])

In other words, if we obtain such spiritual breakthrough whenever we share Jesus Christ with sinners, our message goes with power and with low resistance from them. And it becomes so easy for us to bring the sinner to Christ. When we pray for the sick or about anything, the presence of

God around us makes all the difference. This is indeed great spiritual encouragement.

Please note these words from the pen of inspiration:

> When Jesus bowed on the banks of Jordan at his baptism, Heaven was opened to his prayer in behalf of humanity. The Spirit, in the form of a dove of burnished gold encircled his head, and a voice from Heaven said, "This is my beloved Son, in whom I am well pleased." What does this say to us? It says to every poor tempted soul, Heaven is opened to the prayers of humanity. Christ has encircled the fallen race with his human arm, and with his divine arm he has grasped the throne of the Infinite. Through the merit of Christ, Heaven is opened to man. (White, *Signs of the Times*, July 15, 1889, par. 8)

According to the testimony shared by Pastor John, we are told what the enemy of human souls does to those, "who have broken through in prayer." He said:

> They marked such people and studied them. They would dig up everything they could find about them, so they knew their weaknesses. When someone overcame them in prayer and broke through, they would communicate with other spirits saying "Target him with this and this and this. These are his weaknesses." So when this person walks out of the prayer closet, the spirit of prayer is upon him, the presence is with him, his spirit are high, the joy of the Lord is his strength. As he goes the enemy tries to bring those things that can distract him from focusing on the Lord.
>
> If his weakness is in the area of temper, the enemy will cause people to do things which can make him angry. If he is not sensitive to the Holy Spirit, and he allows himself to lose his temper, he takes his eyes off the Lord. He gets angry, he feels so furious, then after a few minutes, he wants to put it behind him and move forward in the joy of the Lord; however, he doesn't feel joyful anymore. He tries to feel good again, but can't. Why? While he was yielding to the temptation, they were worked hard to close the opening above him. Once they have restored the rock, the presence is cut off. The person does not cease being a child of God. But that extra anointing on his life, the presence that worked apart from his own effort, is cut off. (http://1ref.us/rm, [accessed 2/27/2019])

In other words, the devil cuts us off from the throne of mercy, although the person does not cease being a child of God. But that extra anointing that goes on in his life, that presence that could do things without his manipulating anything, it's just cut off. From the testimony we learn that if a man's weakness is in the area of sexual immorality,

> The enemy will prepare people or events, something to suddenly arouse his passion to move towards the temptation. And if the man yields to the temptation and opens his mind to receive and entertain its thoughts, when he is through and wants to move in the anointing, he discovers it is no longer there. You might say, "That's not fair." Just remember what the Bible says, "Put on the helmet of salvation. Put on the breastplate of righteousness." We normally do not understand the part these weapons of warfare play in our lives. But remember what Jesus told us to pray towards the end of the Lord's Prayer, "Take us not into temptation, but deliver us from the evil one" (Matt. 6:13).
>
> Every time you have a breakthrough in prayer, remember you are still a weak human being. Remember you have not yet been made perfect. Say to the Lord, Lord, I've enjoyed this time of prayer, but as I walk out into the world, lead me not into temptation. Don't allow me to walk into the devil's trap. I know the enemy is setting a trap out there. I don't know what form it is going to take, and I know I am still weak in certain areas. Given the right circumstances, I will yield to temptation. Protect me, Lord. When you see me turning the corner where the trap has been set, cause me to turn the other way. Intervene, O lord. Don't let me move only in my own strength and ability. Deliver me from the evil one.
>
> God is able to do it. He is able. That is why things happen sometimes. All you need to say is, "Thank you, Jesus." That is why Apostle Paul wrote in the book of Thessalonians, "Thank God in everything for that is the will of God in Christ for you" (1 Thess. 5:18).
>
> Some things are not good. They are painful, and we wonder why God would allow them. But if we only knew what He is saving us from, we would thank Him. When we have learned to trust the Lord, we just thank Him in everything.
>
> The man said that when prayer breaks through like that, the answer will always come. He said he did not know of a single case in where prayer broke through and the answer did not come. He said the answer always came, but that in most cases, it never reached the person who asked for it. Why? The Battle in the heavenlies, he said that after they succeeded in cutting of the open heaven and restoring the rock,

they would watch the person, and wait because they know the answer would definitely come. (http://1ref.us/rm, [accessed 2/27/2019])

That is why we are told from the pen of inspiration that, "heavenly agencies have to contend with hindrances before the purpose of God is fulfilled in its time" (White, Letter 201, 1899).

"[Cyrus] the [Persian] monarch had resisted the impressions of the Spirit of God during the three weeks while Daniel was fasting and praying, but Heaven's Prince, the archangel, Michael, was sent to turn the heart of the stubborn king to take some decided action to answer the prayer of Daniel" (White, *Review and Herald,* Feb. 8, 1881).

So friends, the battle is always intense, and when the host of darkness overpowers an angel of God by simply displacing him from his subject, by way of causing the human to sin, and live an indifferent life, he disconnects him or her from their angelic guard. "Then the enemy would send his own angel to them as an angel of light. That's how deceptions come- false visions and false prophecies, false leading or guidance in the spirit and the making of all kinds of wrong decisions. And many times this person is open to all kinds of attack and bondages" (http://1ref.us/rm, [accessed 2/27/2019]).

"It is time for every one of us to decide whose side we are on. The agencies of Satan will work with every mind that will allow itself to be worked by him. But there are also heavenly agencies waiting to communicate the bright rays of the glory of God to all that are willing to receive Him. It is truth that we want, precious truth in all its loveliness. Truth will bring liberty and gladness" (White, *The SDA Bible Commentary,* vol. 4, p. 1154.2).

The Shaking of the Last Days

Confirming his account, an inspired writer, who too was privileged to get a shocking glimpse into the spiritual realm, also wrote:

> I saw some, with strong faith and agonizing cries, pleading with God. Their countenances were pale, and marked with deep anxiety, expressive of their internal struggle. Firmness and great earnestness was expressed in their countenances; large drops of perspiration fell from their foreheads. Now and then their faces would light up with the marks of God's approbation, and again the same solemn, earnest, anxious look would settle upon them.
>
> Evil angels crowded around, pressing darkness upon them to shut out Jesus from their view, that their eyes might be drawn to the darkness that surrounded them, and thus they be led to distrust God,

and murmur against Him. Their only safety was in keeping their eyes directed upward. Angels of God had charge over His people, and as the poisonous atmosphere of evil angels was pressed around these anxious ones, the heavenly angels were continually wafting their wings over them to scatter the thick darkness....

...I was shown those whom I had before seen weeping and praying in agony of spirit. The company of guardian angels around them had been doubled, and they were clothed with armor from their head to their feet. They moved in exact order, like a company of soldiers. Their countenances expressed the severe conflict which they had endured, the agonizing struggle they had passed through. Yet their features, marked with severe internal anguish, now shone with the light and glory of heaven. They had obtained the victory, and it called forth from them the deepest gratitude, and holy, sacred joy.

The numbers of this company had lessened. Some had been shaken out and left by the way. The careless and indifferent, who did not join with those who prized victory and salvation enough to perseveringly plead and agonize for it, did not obtain it, and they were left behind in darkness, and their places were immediately filled by others taking hold of the truth and coming into the ranks. Evil angels still pressed around them, but could have no power over them.

I heard those clothed with the armor speak forth the truth with great power. It had effect. Many had been bound; some wives by their husbands, and some children by their parents. The honest who had been prevented from hearing the truth now eagerly laid hold upon it. All fear of their relatives was gone, and the truth alone was exalted to them. They had been hungering and thirsting for truth; it was dearer and more precious than life. I asked what had made this great change. An angel answered, "It is the latter rain, the refreshing from the presence of the Lord, the loud cry of the third angel." (White, *Christian Experience and Teachings of Ellen G. White*, pp. 175–177)

Beloved, now that we have received this revelation from the Lord, all we have to do is put it into practice. We have once more understood why several of our prayers remain unanswered. We again comprehend why we sometimes have the impression that demons are stronger than we are. The Lord, through this revelation, has just reminded us of the need for every child of God to devote at least one hour every day to this warfare without interruption.

Let us stand up now and fight while correcting all the errors of the past. Let us restart the warfare anew today. Let us ensure that our hour of battle is never again disturbed. For this reason, it is necessary to turn off all phones and avoid any distractions, whatever they may be, during this time of prayer. Make all your efforts to spend some time with the Lord without any interruptions or distractions, and you will see great results in your life and throughout the whole church.

THE BENEFITS OF FASTING

First of all, what should we not do when we fast? The scripture says, **"Moreover, when ye FAST, be not, as the hypocrites, of a sad countenance: for they disfigure their faces, that they may appear unto men that they fast"** (Matt. 6:16).

We are not to look for praise or attention when we are fasting, we are not to bow our heads like we're suffering or think of self. Isaiah the prophet wrote:

> [Is] not this the fast that I have chosen? To loose the bands of wickedness, to undo the heavy burdens, and to let the oppressed go free, and that ye break every yoke? [Is it] not to deal thy bread to the hungry, and that thou bring the poor that are cast out to thy house? when thou seest the naked, that thou cover him; and that thou hide not thyself from thine own flesh? Then shall thy light break forth as the morning, and thine health shall spring forth speedily: and thy righteousness shall go before thee; the glory of the LORD shall be thy rereward. Then shalt thou call, and the LORD shall answer; thou shalt cry, and he shall say, Here I [am]. (Isa. 58:6–9)

What are some of those things we should fast for?

1. **Satanic Affliction** (Matt. 17:18, 21)
2. **Heart Cleansing** (White, *Counsels on Diet and Foods,* p. 187.6)
3. **Imprisonment** (White, *The Acts of the Apostles,* p. 144.2)
4. **Meeting an Opponent** (White, *Testimonies for the Church vol. 1,* p. 624.2)
5. **To Understand the Truth** (White, *Counsels on Diet and Foods,* p. 187.2)
6. **Fasting for the Sick and Dying** (White, *Patriarchs and Prophets,* p. 722.3)
7. **Ministerial Ordination** (Acts 14:23; White, *The Acts of the Apostles,* p. 160.2)

8. **Facing Persecution** (Esther 4:3, 16–17; White, *Prophets and Kings*, p. 601.1)
9. **Deliverance From Spiritualism** (White, *Testimonies for the Church vol 1*, p. 343.2)
10. **For Wisdom** (White, *Counsels on Diet and Foods*, p. 188.1)
11. **Treatment of Disease** (White, *Counsels on Diet and Foods*, pp. 189.4, 190.3)
12. **To Overcome Appetite** (White, *Counsels on Diet and Foods*, p. 400.3)
13. **Sins Of Oppression** (Isa. 58:6, 7; White, *The SDA Bible Commentary*, vol. 4, p. 1150.1)
14. **The Holy Spirit's Comfort** (White, *The Desire of Ages*, p. 277.4)

Does fasting require a person to abstain 100% from food? "Now and onward till the close of time the people of God should be more earnest, more wide-awake, not trusting in their own wisdom, but in the wisdom of their Leader. They should set aside days for **FASTING AND PRAYER.** Entire abstinence from food may not be required, but they should eat sparingly of the most simple food" (White, *Counsels on Diet and Foods*, p. 188.4).

It is not advisable to impose upon ourselves certain kinds of fasting that the scriptures do not teach, such as popular "Ninety-day Juice Fast." "So much liquid taken into the stomach was not healthful, and that all who subsisted on such a diet placed a great tax upon the kidneys, and so much watery substance debilitated the stomach" (White, *Counsels on Diet and Foods*, p. 105.2). "Soft or liquid foods are less wholesome than dry foods, which require thorough mastication" (White, *The Ministry of Healing*, p. 301.4).

What about a fruit fast for several days? "A fruit diet for a few days has often brought great relief to brain workers" (White, *Counsels and Diet and Foods*, p. 189.3).

"We are mortal, and must supply ourselves with food that will give proper sustenance to the body" (White, *Counsels on Diet and Foods*, p. 92.3).

"Grains, fruits, nuts, and vegetables, in proper combination, contain all the elements of nutrition; and when properly prepared, they constitute the diet that best promotes both physical and mental strength" (White, *Education*, p. 204.3).

What about the forty-day fasting? "You are not called upon to fast forty days. The Lord bore that fast for you in the wilderness of temptation.

There would be no virtue in such a fast; but there is virtue in the blood of Christ" (White, *Counsels and Diet and Foods,* p. 189.1).

What about eating only once-a-day fast? "I have been informed that you have taken but one meal a day for a period of time ... You will surely decrease in strength and your mind become unbalanced unless you change your course of abstemious diet" (White, *Counsels on Diet and Foods,* p. 191.1–2). In other words, this kind of once-a-day fasting should not be practiced for more than a week.

What about a no-food fast for many days? "Fast for a meal or two ... Many times a short period of entire abstinence from food, followed by simple, moderate eating, has led to recovery through nature's own recuperative effort" (White, *The Ministry of Healing,* p. 235.2).

"There are some who would be benefited more by **ABSTINENCE FROM FOOD FOR A DAY OR TWO EVERY WEEK** than by any amount of treatment or medical advice. **TO FAST ONE DAY A WEEK** would be of incalculable benefit to them" (White, *Counsels on Diet and Foods,* p. 189.4).

What type of fasting is to be done now during the anti-typical Day of Atonement? "Once a year, on the great day of atonement, the priest entered the most holy place for the cleansing of the sanctuary ... every man was required to afflict his soul while this work of atonement was going forward. All business was to be laid aside and the whole congregations of Israel were to spend the day in solemn humiliation before God, with prayer, fasting, and deep searching of heart" (White, *The Great Controversy,* p. 419.1, 3).

If we are now in the anti-typical Day of Atonement, what is the fast that we are required to have today? "The true fasting which should be recommended to all, is abstinence from every stimulating kind of food, and the proper use of wholesome, simple food, which God has provided in abundance" (White, *Counsels on Diet and Foods,* p. 90.1).

BENEFITS FROM FASTING ACCORDING TO MEDICAL SCIENCE:
1. **Helps Brain Diseases** (http://1ref.us/rn, [accessed 2/27/2019])
2. **Improves Alzheimer's**
3. **Enhances Mental Acuity**
4. **Improves the Function of the Heart**
5. **Reduces Depression, Tension, and Anxiety**
6. **Promotes Detoxification**
7. **Gives the Digestive System Rest**

8. **Helps Reduce Inflammation**
9. **Reduces Blood Pressure**
10. **Helps Clear up the Skin**
11. **Restores Taste**
12. **Lessens the Desire for Addictions**
13. **Promotes Rapid Weight Loss**
    (http://1ref.us/ro, [accessed 2/27/2019])

May the Lord Jesus bless you and renew your zeal for Him. Amen!

CHAPTER 9

ANGELS AND DEMONS

In this chapter, we shall take a spectacular look at the subject of spiritualism and its inroad into Christianity. According to the *Concise Oxford English Dictionary*, spiritualism is defined as "a system of belief or religious practice based on supposed communication with the spirits of the dead, especially through mediums."

The word "spiritualism" is not found in the Bible, but there is a general accord that spiritualism is based upon the belief in the natural immortality of the human soul, and that the spirit which leaves the fleshly body at death can and does return to communicate with the living through a medium. In God's Word, we are told that "After the flood as men began to migrate from the east they found a plain in the land of Shinar; and they dwelt there" (Gen. 11:2).

The Bible also says they were led by one powerfully built man by name Nimrod. "And Cush begat Nimrod: he began to be a mighty one in the earth. He was a mighty hunter before the LORD: wherefore it is said, Even as Nimrod the mighty hunter before the LORD" (10:8–10). At that time, the threat of wild animals was the problem the people were continuously facing, so Nimrod became not only their protector, but also their king, and he was a famous leader in worldly affairs among these primitive people.

> *Thus, the belief in the immortality of the human soul was born among these early inhabitants of the earth, in line with Satan's first lie: "Ye shall not surely die"*

Not long after Nimrod died, according to ancient legend, Queen Semiramis, the wife of this famous king, announced that her husband's spirit had become immortal and took possession of the sun. Hence, he became Bealt-samon, the lord of heaven, the sun god. Thus, the belief in the immortality of the human soul was born among these early inhabitants of the earth, in line with Satan's first lie: "Ye shall not surely die" (3:4).

Here is the origin of the practice of spiritualism, with its act of communication with the dead. God's warning is, "There shall not be found among you *any one* that… useth divination, *or* an observer of times, or an enchanter, or a witch, Or a charmer, or a consulter with familiar spirits, or a wizard, or a necromancer. For all that do these things *are* an abomination unto the LORD: and because of these abominations the LORD thy God doth drive them out from before thee". (Deut. 18:10–12).

"Regard not them that have familiar spirits, neither seek after wizards, to be defiled by them: I *am* the LORD your God" (Lev. 19:31).

Modern Spiritualism

It is interesting to note that the modern spiritualism movement began on March 31, 1848, when Kate and Margareta Fox, ages 11 and 13, heard mysterious rapping on the wall of their house. "The unseen intelligence then indicated that it was the spirit of a murdered peddler whose body has been buried in the cellar. It was seeking a human instrument through whom to acquaint the world with the facts of his mysterious disappearance and to prove that his spirit still lived" (Froom 1965, p. 1053).

The news drew millions. Many were swept into spiritualism, and interest began to grow. A code of communication was developed, and there began to appear what looked like spiritual manifestations. The world's attention was caught, and people became more captivated by spiritualism.

Though the first spiritualist congregation, as an individual church, was established in Sturgis, Michigan in 1858, it was not until 1893 that actions were taken to declare the entire movement to be a church. Thenceforth, spiritualist congregations spread everywhere, with ordained ministers, church manuals, hymnals, yearbooks, etc.

Satan's Plan for Conquest

Ten years after the birth of modern spiritualism movement, in the early spring of 1858, a young Christian lady Ellen had an extremely very powerful and notable vision, with her husband James they were on the road again. On the weekend of March 13 and 14, they attended meetings at Lovett's Grove, in Ohio.

On Sunday afternoon, the 14th, a funeral was conducted by James in the schoolhouse where the earlier meeting of the weekend had been held. After he had spoken, Ellen rose to speak words of comfort and was taken off in vision. Lasting two hours, during which time she was given a panoramic view of the great controversy between Christ and Satan that has spanned the ages of sin.

She reveals that "through the two great errors, the immortality of the soul and Sunday sacredness Satan will bring the people under his deception" (White 1911, p. 588). "A belief in spiritual manifestations," she said, will "open the door to seducing spirits, and doctrines of devils, and thus the influence of evil angels will be felt in the churches" (pp. 603, 604).

In her vision of 1858, she was shown a number of unmistakable identifying marks, fourteen of which we will delineate as separate aspects of Satan's plan for the conquest of humanity. Each one of them will enable us to distinguish and recognize spiritualism in those places where it has infiltrated religious and secular society. This is how the aspects manifest:

1. Through spiritualism, many false Christ and prophets will become public figures (see PP 686.1).
2. It will appear that the whole world will be "aboard" the spiritualistic movement (see FLB 319.4; EW 263.1).
3. It will be considered blasphemy to speak against its manifestation (EW 86.4).
4. It will claim that all miracles wrought by Jesus were merely psychic manifestations (see GC 552, 556).
5. The movement will closely imitate nominal Christianity (see GC 588.2).
6. Through its power, miracles will be wrought, and the sick will be healed (see 4SP 405.3).
7. Protestants will be foremost in grasping the hand of spiritualism (see GC 588.1).
8. Spiritualism will work side by side with the preaching of the gospel (see GC 588).
9. It will be regarded as a grand movement for the conversion of the world (see GC 588.3).
10. Spiritualism will profess to present a new and more exalted system of religious faith (see GC 589.1).
11. It will advocate the immortality of the soul and Sunday sacredness (see GC 588).

12. Spiritualistic manifestations will be accepted into the churches (see GC 588.2).
13. The Ten Commandments will be taught to be a dead letter; the Bible will no longer be regarded as the foundation of faith (see GC 558.1).
14. Seducing spirits will introduce doctrines of devils in the last days (see 8MR 345.3).

Spiritualism and Christianity

Spiritualism, Satan's plan of conquest, has already become an accepted form of worship. Many plans for how to infiltrate Christian churches were hatched. It was first adopted by Catholicism and then accepted by apostate Protestantism. In order to infiltrate Christianity, Satan adopted a list of general definitions, prepared to suit the varied tastes and capacities of those whom he could ruin. One of its advocates, Shaw Desmond, is convinced that the impact of the infiltration of spiritualism into the Christian churches will more than likely result in the unification of the various denominations and the Christian religion becoming the religion of the psychic. Religion and science, he says, "will not only talk but also walk together" (1954, pp. 269, 270).

Believing that the church itself was born at Pentecost in a rush of wind, flame of fire, and spirit-filled utterances, spiritualism senses the benefit of a slight change of name—spiritualism for Pentecostalism, medium for prophet, clairvoyance for discernment of the spirit, psychic phenomenon for miracles, spirit light for tongues of fire. One of the leading advocates of spiritualism, Reverend D. Monna Berry asserts, "Modern spiritualism is a powerful ally of true Christianity" (*What Is Spiritualism?*, p. 38).

The National Spiritualist Association of Churches listed the various ways in which their spiritual power manifests itself:

> The **Phenomena of Spiritualism** consists of Prophecy, Clairvoyance, Clairaudience, Gift of Tongues, Laying on of Hands, Healing, Visions, Trance, Apports, Levitation, Raps, Automatic and Independent Writings and Paintings, Voice, Materialization, Photography, Psychometry and any other manifestation proving the continuity of life as demonstrated through the Physical and Spiritual senses and faculties of man. (http://1ref.us/r1, [accessed 11/15/2018])

This places the aforementioned psychic medium in direct relationship to the teachings of spiritualism.

Charismatic Movement

It is foretold in the Scriptures that "in the latter times some shall depart from the faith, giving heed to seducing spirits, and doctrines of devils" (1 Tim. 4:1). Paul pointed to the special working of Satan through spiritualism as an event to take place immediately before the second advent of Christ. Speaking of Christ's second coming, he declared that it is "after the working of Satan with all power and signs and lying wonders" (2 Thess. 2:9).

Paul, further describing the dangers to which the church was to be exposed in the last days, said that as there were false prophets who led Israel into sin, so there will be false teachers. "For such *are* false apostles, deceitful workers, transforming themselves into the apostles of Christ. And no marvel; for Satan himself is transformed into an angel of light. Therefore *it is* no great thing if his ministers also be transformed as the ministers of righteousness; whose end shall be according to their works" (2 Cor. 11:13–15).

The charismatic Pentecostal revival we see today began in 1900, during a watch night service in Kansas City. Starting December 31, 1900, and ending on what was technically the first day of the twentieth century, Charles Parham of Topeka, Kansas laid his hand on Agnes Ozman. She began speaking in tongues, and the movement was born.

Another "fascinating chain of events led to the famous Azusa Street revival of 1906, which began under the ministry of William Seymour" (Wagner 1979, p. 20).

"Spiritualist and mediums from numerous occult societies of Los Angeles contributed their séances and trances to the service of the Azusa street revival" (Synan 1971, p. 110).

"The Pentecostal movement gained high visibility and a momentum that has never slacked as we can see today" (Wagner 1979, p. 20).

Although the majority of Christians were not prepared for this; "some of the Pentecostal denominations began to gain respectability by joining organizations such as the National Association of Evangelicals. Thereby they partially neutralized the opinion held by some that Pentecostalism was false sect" (p. 21).

A major outcome was the hearty acceptance of the charismatic movement by the Episcopal, Presbyterians, United Methodist, and many other Protestant churches, and even the Roman Catholic Church. It is interesting to note that the people who led these churches into Pentecostalism were all spiritualist mediums.

The Spread of Pentecostalism

Within Pentecostalism's first twenty years, missionaries had developed churches in China, India, Japan, Egypt, Liberia, Angola, Brazil, and Mexico. Pentecostal missions in Africa flourished because, unlike the American missionaries who tried to destroy the African worldview of supernaturalism, Pentecostalism took it seriously and made sense out of it by assuming "that there is a supernatural connection to God who acts through dreams, visions, healing, and other divine interventions" (Patheos, http://1ref.us/qu, [accessed 11/15/2018]).

This "here and now" perspective of Pentecostalism does not look forward to a new world where God will restore life to His original plan. Instead, it seeks to make this world a better place so that God's people can live in it and "possess their possession." This perhaps explains why its worldview, expressed through teaching and preaching, places significant emphasis on contemporary temporal issues such as prosperity, empowerment, success, and healing.

In its formative years (1906–1940), American Pentecostalism was organized around established denominations to stabilize leadership, codify doctrine, and provide infrastructure for missions, education, and evangelism. However, in response to the perceived loss of spiritual vibrancy that threatened to set in, "independent evangelists began advocating for a renewal of the church, outside the established denominations, which they called human institutions that quenched the Spirit" (Patheos, http://1ref.us/qv, [accessed 11/15/2018]).

This anti-denominational sentiment saw the emergence of leaders like Kenneth Hagin and Oral Roberts who, through theological and technological innovations such as televangelism, brought the Pentecostal practice to a mass audience. This phenomenon was later sustained by other powerful western Pentecostal televangelists of the twentieth and twenty-first centuries, such as Jimmy Swaggart, Benny Hinn, Myles Munroe, Charles G. Scott, etc.

Observable Strengths of Pentecostalism

1. Simple, handy, and affordable publications for nurturing church members
2. Simplified liturgy that enhances congregational participation without much rigor
3. Use of simple congregational choruses that facilitate quick learning and participation in singing

4. Focus on meeting the felt needs of church members here and now
5. Attentive to identify and follow up on visitors and new interests
6. Zeal for God and godly activities
7. Commitment of church members to whatever their pastors say or teach
8. Love for their churches
9. Respect for and confidence in their pastors and leaders, in spite of their humanness

Observable Weaknesses

1. Shallow knowledge and use of the Bible
2. Limited *kerygma* ("things preached"); sermons are more motivational talks and entertainment
3. Poor biblical hermeneutics (interpretation) and Bible-based theology
4. Minimizing the need for adequate theological training for ministers (under the guise that the Holy Spirit is their Teacher)
5. Tendency toward deifying and idolizing their leaders and pastors, whom they perceive to be nearly immortal and out of this world
6. Exaggerating the power and capacity of humanity (tendency to exalt human beings to the status of God)
7. Exalting and celebrating success with little or no room for failure; hence, popular expressions such as "Failure is not your (my) portion"; "You are (I am) a success."
8. Believing and teaching that no harm can come near the child of God
9. Difficulty in accepting and dealing with negative situations like problems, failure, terminal illnesses, and death, with strong accentuations during prayer such as:
   a. "Failure is not your (my) portion"
   b. "Your (my) body is not made for sickness"
   c. "You (I) shall not die, but live"
   d. "Death is not your (my) portion"

Today this experience has assumed another dimension through the introduction of a new wave of discipline called spiritual formation.

Spiritual Formation

What is spiritual formation? According to the Course of Study School of Ohio (COSSO), "SPIRITUAL FORMATION is a lifelong process of growing closer to God" (http://1ref.us/qw, [accessed 11/15/2018]). With this definition, one would assume that it's the same subject as the one addressed in chapter 3 of this book. However, it isn't.

This is a new wave of spirituality that has, over the last few years, merged into Christianity with rapidity, spreading throughout the various denominations. The subject is being taught in all the Christian seminaries around the world. When carefully and candidly assessed, one will notice that it does not in any way reflect true Christianity, and therefore does not merit the definition ascribed to it.

This is a practice in which people subjectively bring themselves into a trancelike state, and during such a state, they receive information of various kinds, and none of the information is filtered according to their sense of values or worth because their very reasoning power is bypassed.

Those involved in this practice often talk about activating one's sixth sense, also referred to as extrasensory perception (ESP), the ability to perceive information without using the five physical senses. There are several types of ESP.

"**Here are the major types of ESP in a nutshell:**

- **Precognition** — The ability to see into the future.
- **Retrocognition** — The ability to see into the distant past.
- **Clairvoyance** — The ability to see events without being physically present.
- **Mediumship** — The ability to communicate with spiritual world and talk to the deceased.
- **Clairsentience** — The ability to feel the emotions of others
- **Clairaudience** — The ability to receive messages and information through "psychic hearing".
- **Telepathy** — The ability to read the minds of others and know what they're thinking.
- **Clairalience** — The ability to get psychic impressions from the sense of smell.
- **Clairgustance** — The paranormal ability to taste a substance without putting it in mouth"

(Psychics 4 Today, http://1ref.us/qx, [accessed 11/15/2018]).

Does this not look very much like the old styles of worship that have existed for many centuries among the various Eastern religions?

Hindu Spirituality

Spiritual formation originated among the Hindus as one of their elements of public worship in their temples, as well as the rituals accompanying their home worship. To the Hindu, the entire universe and everything within it is God. In other words, God is an impersonal force that constitutes everything in existence. There is no difference between creature and creator, as both are one.

The goal of all Hindus is to achieve self-realization. This is the realization that they themselves are a god force. When self-realization, known as a state of God-consciousness, is achieved, it is said that the person has gained control of his or her spirit. The human spirit is considered to be a god force.

Yoga, one of the physical exercises in spiritual formation, is a vital part of Hindu discipline. Shiva, the Hindu god is traditionally regarded as the founder of yoga. The purpose of yoga is to bring the practitioner into union with the god force or universal soul (Shiva, the Hindu god). The act is practiced through deep meditation, concentration, controlled breathing exercises, and certain physical postures.

Under this practice of mantra, otherwise known as contemplative prayer, there is a rapid repetition of a series of words or sounds. In fact, "Mantra meditation is an essential practice in many forms of yoga, helping to deepen inner awareness. It is also a ritual used in many Eastern religions, including Hinduism, Buddhism, Sikhism and Jainism" (Yogapedia, http://1ref.us/qy, [accessed 11/15/2018]).

Mantras are a direct doorway, opening up the person to the entrance of a spirit. "A mantra is a syllable, word, or phrase that is repeated during meditation.… Most mantra meditation techniques have two essential components: mindfulness meditation and mantra recitation or chanting" (Mindworks, http://1ref.us/qz [accessed 11/15/2018]).

The practice has two purposes to accomplish:

1. Produce a mystical state, which is a trance, in which the mind is empty (blanked out). This, in turn, places the person in direct contact with the invisible spirit world.
2. "Embody" a spiritual being. As the words are spoken, the being comes into existence and enters the person performing the mantra.

Zen Buddhism

Zen Buddhism is a sect primarily practiced in China and Japan. This religion stresses meditation as the means of understanding true reality. "The practice of Zen meditation or Zazen (座禅 - *za* meaning sitting, and *Zen* meaning meditation in Japanese), is the core of Zen Buddhism" (http://1ref.us/r0, [accessed 11/15/2018]).

Buddhism was founded in 624 BC in Lumbini, India by a former Hindu adherent. "Buddhism teaches the way to perfect goodness and wisdom without a personal God; the highest knowledge without a revelation, the possibility of redemption without a vicarious redeemer, a salvation in which everyone is his own savior" (Watch Tower Bible and Tract Society of Pennsylvania 1990, p. 145).

Zen Buddhism stands in contrast to other forms of Buddhism by rejecting the worship of deities, as well as religious authorities and rituals, asserting that enlightenment and spiritual liberation come through meditation and intuition, rather than from the Buddhist scriptures. One of Buddhism's ultimate goals is to attain nirvana, the state of perfect peace and enlightenment, freed from desire and suffering. Zen teaches that in every person there is a nature of Buddha. In other words, everyone is capable of becoming a Buddha—an enlightened one.

For any soul to attain enlightenment, he or she must undergo *bhavana*, which means "development," "cultivating," or "producing" in the sense of "calling into existence." This is an experience every Buddhist attains through meditation. Zen Buddhism believes that every person has tremendous energy within oneself, while to the Hindus this energy is called the god force. Buddhists say this energy is more powerful than an atomic bomb and a fantastic resource to achieve the highest goal of enlightenment.

Zen Transcendental Meditation

Transcendental meditation is a yoga-derived technique whereby one can achieve mental and spiritual tranquility and discover the meaning of existence, as well as develop an awareness of one's true self. Those practicing transcendental meditation generally sit in a yoga position with eyes closed as they chant and concentrate on an ancient mantra (contemplative prayer). This is practiced twice daily, morning and evening, for thirty minutes.

In chanting the mantra, the mind does not dwell on the meaning of the word but concentrates on the sound. As conscious thoughts try to enter the mind, they are replaced by the mantra until all thinking is gradually eliminated and a trance-like mental state of quietness and serenity is achieved. Through concentration on the sound of the word, practitioners relax mentally, blotting out self-concern, conscious thought, and awareness, until they reach cosmic consciousness.

This same idea that we must prepare ourselves to be capable of manifesting the divine presence is the very foundation of every Eastern religion, including Buddhism. That is, to make significant spiritual progress, we must practice meditation. Can you see that spiritual formation is a discipline practiced in Hinduism, Buddhism, and New Age religion? Furthermore, today there is an inroad of this Eastern mysticism into Christianity.

Catholicism

Among the first to use an Eastern form of meditation as a means of seeking union with God were the monks who lived in isolation in the Egyptian desert in the fourth century. "'The first profess Christian monks... practiced a discipline of purification and meditation as a way to unite with God,' writes Rosemary Ellen Guiley. 'Their techniques either were borrowed from the East or were spontaneous rediscoveries of the same (methods). The Desert Fathers had the Christian equivalents of mantras; phrases from the scriptures repeated either silently or verbally'" (Missett 2005, p. 144).

These meditative techniques were not only known to ascetic monks in the Egyptian desert but to the Vatican as well. St. Bernard of Clairvaux (1090–1153), a mystical Catholic priest who experienced spiritual visions, wrote four books entitled *Meditation for Pope Eugene III*. He described meditation as "mental prayer, by which one converses with God and May perhaps attain a vision of God and union with him even in this life" (Ibid.).

Ignatius of Loyola

Ignatius of Loyola was born in 1491 into a wealthy Spanish home during the reign of King Ferdinand and Queen Isabella. He was the youngest of thirteen children raised in a family culture of high Catholic piety, but lax morals. Trained to be a knight, he joined the Spanish army, and in May 1521, at the Battle of Pamplona, while fighting against France, a tiny band of Spanish soldiers trying to defend the town was all ready to surrender, except Ignatius. He would hold off the French singlehandedly. However, a French cannonball shattered his leg and put an end to his stand. Nevertheless, the French admired his courage. They carried him on a stretcher back home to his castle of Loyola.

After much effort to properly set his broken leg failed, it remained shorter than the other, and Ignatius limped for the rest of his life. While recovering, he spent a lot of time reading mystical literature, which led him to leave behind his life of wealth and live as a hermit. He devoted himself to asceticism and the examples of others of like mind, such as Francis of Assisi and St. Dominic, and adopted their meditational lifestyles and spiritual disciplines.

Ignatius gained personal experience as he practiced transcendental meditation and took stock of Eastern mysticism. He recorded his experiences in a notebook and would soon find his jottings helpful in guiding others. His concept of God, in these mystical experiences, was pantheistic. He also developed what is today called spiritual exercises, which are the textual foundation for modern spiritual formation. From these spiritual exercises come the most important practices of the *examen*, a daily practice of prayer, and *medita*, essential to spiritual formation.

Ignatius' experience was in mysticism, and he taught it to all those enlisted in the Jesuit order, which he founded. In his book *The Jesuit*, Malachi Martin wrote of Ignatius' passion for mysticism. "Ignatius Loyola presumed that every Jesuit would have this same perpetual preoccupation with finding God in all things" (1988, pp. 206, 207).

The spiritual exercises of Ignatius of Loyola, the founder of the Jesuit order, are the foundation upon which modern spiritual formation is built. The theology taught in all spiritual formation seminars is derived from Ignatius of Loyola. The languages, phrases, and terminology that describe the mission of the teachings are all from his spiritual exercises.

The leading advocates and instructors of spiritual formation have repeatedly declared that it originated over many centuries within ancient Hinduism and Buddhism, and through the ascetic monks of the Egyptian desert, it seeped into the medieval Catholic Church and became the basic teaching in Ignatius' spiritual exercises. They are not ashamed of that fact.

One of the Buddhist instructors at a Catholic college wrote the following:

> When I teach courses on Buddhism in Boston College, a Catholic university, I try to show many connections between doctrine and practice not just to help students understand Buddhist traditions but also to point them toward analogous integrations of thought and spiritual practice in Christian traditions, and perhaps in their own lives.... many Christians, Jews, and others are seeking in Buddhism the means to reintroduce themselves to their own spiritual lives and traditions in light of the Buddhist emphasis on connecting philosophical reflection to spiritual discipline....

...Christian theology students [Catholic priests] in my classes on Buddhism often find themselves looking back into the history of Christianity to explore analogous integrations of doctrinal learning and practice to further inform their own theological process. (Religious Studies News, http://1ref.us/r3, [accessed 11/15/2018])

With this, you can see that this whole exercise traces its origin to ancient Hinduism and Buddhism through the ascetic monks of the Egyptian desert. The Roman Catholics have used these practices for centuries. They originally came from the Eastern religions, especially the mysterious religions of Asia Minor. Monasteries and nunneries continue to provide special instructions in the meditative and contemplative disciplines.

Also, "spiritual retreats" have been familiar among Roman Catholics who seek relief from the stress of everyday care. Their religion does not provide comfort in Christ, and they gladly turn to other things. However, these traditions are neither first-century Christian nor biblical in origin. They are Catholic, adopted from pagan religious practices. And this is the same spiritual formation now entering Protestantism.

Jesuit Pantheistic Spirituality

As of today, spiritual formation has spread so rapidly through the churches that it is now even being taught in Protestant seminaries. It's interesting to note that biblical spirituality encompasses the entirety of the Christian life. It's a holistic approach to faith that includes our beliefs and practices, as well as the way we live our everyday lives. It is living a new life of obedience to God's Word under the influence of the Holy Spirit through Jesus Christ.

The goal of this spirituality is our transformation into the loving image of God's dear Son and the final union with Him in His eternal home. The Bible says, "And be not conformed to this world: but be ye transformed by the renewing of your mind, that ye may prove what *is* that good, and acceptable, and perfect, will of God" (Rom. 12:2). The Bible speaks of transformation, not formation. It nowhere describes an inward journey to explore the realm of the spirits. The integration of psychological ideas into theological and spiritual contexts, or the exploration of contemplative or mystical practices and experiences in Christianity, is satanic.

It is interesting to note that different forms of spirituality exist between true Christianity and apostate Christianity. The spirituality of true Christianity is rooted in the Bible and the Bible alone, while the spirituality of apostate Christianity is an infiltration of New Age Eastern mysticism with its emerging church and spiritual formation. No matter how enticing the term "spiritual formation" may be, not even a repackaged named like "contemplative spirituality," no matter how well it may be coated in biblical verbiage and claims to be the means of transformation into the character of Christ, its origin is paganism.

Spiritual formation is a satanic deception based on Jesuit pantheistic spirituality. What is the primary goal of spiritual formation? The answer is better understood in the following submission by Chung Kyung, a South Korean Presbyterian minister and professor. Kyung teaches that many religions can lead to God. She states, "I feel like my bowel is Shamanist, my heart is Buddhist, my right brain is Christian... I call it a family of gods and...they are together" (Edwards 1980, p. ???). Kyung shows that the spiritual formation movement is a drive towards global religious unity and the primary, subtle tool the Roman Catholic Church is using to gain control of the whole Christian world.

In the late 1970s and early 1980s, the term "spiritual formation" was hardly known, except for highly specialized references about the Catholic orders. However, today, spiritual formation has spread rapidly through Protestant churches. "Some of the various names under which this Emerging Church is infiltrating the community of faith are ReFormation, Renovare, Rethink; Lighthouse Trails calls it "emerging spirituality." Terms you will find in the Emergent Movement are: Prayer Stations, Breath Prayers, Lectio Divina, Taize, The Silence, Sacred Space, Ancient Prayer Practices, A Thin Place, Spiritual Direction, Ignation Contemplation, Contemplative, Centering, Centering Prayer, Divine Center, Inner light, Mantra, Beyond Words, Spiritual Disciplines, Spiritual Formation, Prayer Labyrinths, Prayer Rooms" (http://1ref.us/r4, [accessed 2/27/2019]).

The above are the various common terms you may be hearing as related to this subject, but the three *major* components of spiritual formation are meditation, centralized prayer (mantra), and visualization. By the practice of these spiritual exercises, Christians are led into New Age mysticism. The first step begins with meditation. In what kind of meditation do they engage?

"Meditating" on the Bible

Practitioners are told to open the Bible, look at one verse, pick a word, keep repeating that word for twenty minutes to an hour, and eventually just sit there in blank-minded silence, which is called "contemplation." This is Hindu/Buddhist *samadhi*.

The Bible never suggests such kind of wild meditation. When Joshua was exhorting the children of Israel, he said, "This book of the law shall not depart out of thy mouth; but thou shalt meditate therein day and night, that thou mayest observe to do according to all that is written therein: for then thou shalt make thy way prosperous, and then thou shalt have good success" (Josh. 1:8).

Biblical meditation is centered on an active mind, not a passive mind. Notice what the focus of meditation should be—the works of God. "I will meditate also of all thy work, and talk of thy doings" (Ps. 77:12). Biblical meditation is thoughtfully spending time reasoning through a biblical subject, rehearsing verses as they connect to the very subject, and mentally reflecting on the deep meaning of each verse as it relates to the subject in question.

It is important to actively engage our whole mind on each subject upon which we are thinking, with a silent prayer asking God to guide us in unraveling the truth as it is in Christ. As the psalmist wrote about his experience and great achievement after meditating on a vital subject, he said, "I have more understanding than all my teachers: for thy testimonies *are* my meditation" (Ps. 119:99).

And it is not just a single word that deserves focus, but all that is written in Scripture. "Blessed *is* the man that walketh not in the counsel of the ungodly, nor standeth in the way of sinners, nor sitteth in the seat of the scornful. But his delight *is* in the law of the LORD; and in his law doth he meditate day and night" (1:1–2).

Please don't meditate on a single word. That kind of meditation has no scriptural support. It is just the opposite of how prayer is defined in the Bible. "Be careful for nothing; but in every thing by prayer and supplication with thanksgiving let your requests be made known unto God" (Phil. 4:6).

"And in that day ye shall ask me nothing. Verily, verily, I say unto you, Whatsoever ye shall ask the Father in my name, he will give *it* you. Hitherto have ye asked nothing in my name: ask, and ye shall receive, that your joy may be full" (John 16:23, 24). These verses and others portray prayer as being comprehensible communication with God, not an esoteric, mystical meditation that bypasses rational, cognitive thinking to give an illusionary experience.

When it comes to taking just one word and repeating it for hours to empty the mind, the Bible describes such prayer as heathen. "But when ye pray, use not vain repetitions, as the heathen *do*: for they think that they shall be heard for their much speaking" (Matt. 6:7).

Centering Prayer

Under this step, the practitioner begins to slow down the breath, controlling the heartbeat in self-inducing hypnosis, silently chants a word repeatedly to help focus the mind while striving to go deep within oneself and concentrates the mind upon nothing (in other words, emptying the mind).

This is how we are taught in the Bible to pray:

After this manner therefore pray ye: Our Father which art in heaven, Hallowed be thy name. Thy kingdom come, Thy will be done in earth, as *it is* in heaven. Give us this day our daily bread. And forgive us our debts, as we forgive our debtors. And lead us not into temptation, but deliver us from evil: For thine is the kingdom, and the power, and the glory, for ever. Amen. (Matthew 6:9–13)

By this, God set a pattern for how we can phrase our prayers to Him.

Visualization

Under this step, all conscious thoughts trying to enter the mind are replaced by a contemplative prayer, which is gradually chanted until all thinking is eliminated and a trance-like mental state of quietness and serenity is achieved. The mind, in an imaginative way, begins to visualize oneself entering deeply into the spiritual realm, the invisible world where diverse spirit beings abide. The soul now begins to see itself "embody" a spiritual being. In other words, a being is seen coming into existence and entering the person using the mantra.

It is at this point that spiritual formation is said to have taken place. The effects of its practices on the mind are remarkably similar to that of hypnosis or the attendance of a séance (for much more on hypnosis, see my eighty-two-page tract, entitled *Occultism in the House of God*).

Last-day Threefold Union

Little by little, Satan has prepared the way for his masterpiece of deception in the development of spiritualism. He has not yet reached the full accomplishment of his designs, but the time is approaching. "I saw three unclean spirits like frogs; ... they are the spirits of devils, working miracles, which go forth unto the kings of the earth and of the whole world, to gather them to the battle of that great day of God Almighty" (Rev. 16:13, 14).

Here the spirits of devils, through spiritual formation, are preparing the rulers and people of the world for a global conflict—the final battle between good and evil. These three satanic mediums are predicted to perform deceiving miracles, which virtually all the inhabitants of the earth will believe to be the power of God. Mystic paganism, Catholicism, and apostate Protestantism, bound together under an ancient discipline called spiritual formation, will take the world by storm.

"Except those who are kept by the power of God, through faith in His word, the whole world will be swept into the ranks of this delusion. The people are fast being lulled to a fatal security, to be awakened only by the outpouring of the wrath of God" (White 1997, p. 23).

Dear friends, stay away from any non-biblical, spiritual disciplines or methods of spiritual formation that are rooted in mysticism, such as contemplative prayer, centering prayer, and the emerging church movement in which these methods are promoted.

> *Dear friends, stay away from any non-biblical, spiritual disciplines or methods of spiritual formation that are rooted in mysticism, such as contemplative prayer, centering prayer, and the emerging church movement in which these methods are promoted*

CHAPTER 10

THE FINAL REVIVAL

When Christ promised to give the Holy Spirit, He was nearing the close of His earthly ministry. He was standing in the shadow of the cross. As He sat on that cool evening while His disciples were listening to Him, He said, "And I will pray the Father, and he shall give you another Comforter that he may abide with you forever" (John 14:16).

As He was speaking, the wind was blowing hard over the mountains round about Jerusalem, rushing down the narrow streets of the city, waving the branches of the trees, tugging at the garments of passersby. It could be heard rattling the shutters and banging the doors of nearby houses. They could not see the wind, but they could feel it and hear its effects. Peter then cited it and said, "and *so is* also the Holy Ghost, whom God hath given to them that obey him" (Acts 5:32). "*Even* the Spirit of truth; whom the world cannot receive, because it seeth him not, neither knoweth him: but ye know him; for he dwelleth with you, and shall be in you" (John 14:17).

Therefore, the first outpouring among Christ's disciples of the Holy Spirit at Pentecost was with impressive, visible, and audible manifestations. The Bible says:

> And when the day of Pentecost was fully come, they were all with one accord in one place. And suddenly there came a sound from heaven as of a rushing mighty wind, and it filled all the house where they were sitting. And there appeared unto them cloven tongues like as of fire, and it sat upon each of them. And they were all filled with the Holy Ghost, and began to speak with other tongues, as the Spirit gave them utterance. (Acts 2:1–4)

The Holy Spirit, assuming the form of tongues of fire, rested upon those assembled. This was an emblem of the gift then bestowed on the disciples, which enabled them to speak with fluency languages with which they had heretofore been unacquainted. The appearance of fire signified the fervent zeal with which the apostles would labor and the power that would attend their work. (White, *The Acts of the Apostles*, p. 39)

Among those gathered in Jerusalem at the time of this event were devout Jews from various nations. During the dispersion, they had been scattered to almost every part of the inhabited world, and in their exile, they learned to speak multiple languages. Many of these Jews were in Jerusalem on this occasion, attending the religious festivals in progress at the time. Thus, every known tongue was represented by those assembled. This diversity of languages would have been a great hindrance to the proclamation of the gospel. God, therefore, in a miraculous manner, supplied the deficiency of the apostles.

By the power of the Holy Spirit, the apostles could proclaim the truths of the gospel abroad, speaking with accuracy the languages of those for whom they were laboring. This miraculous gift was compelling evidence to the world that their commission bore the signet of heaven. From this time forth the language of the disciples was pure, simple, and accurate, whether they spoke in their native tongue or a foreign language.

Peter showed that this demonstration was in direct fulfillment of the prophecy of Joel, wherein he foretold that such power would come upon people to fit them for extraordinary work. The Bible says, "And it shall come to pass afterward, *that* I will pour out my spirit upon all flesh; and your sons and your daughters shall prophesy, your old men shall dream dreams, your young men shall see visions: And also upon the servants and upon the handmaids in those days will I pour out my spirit" (Joel 2:28, 29). With that experience, all the apostles were fully aware that Christ's promise of the Comforter had been fulfilled.

> *By the power of the Holy Spirit, the apostles could proclaim the truths of the gospel abroad, speaking with accuracy the languages of those for whom they were laboring. This miraculous gift was compelling evidence to the world that their commission bore the signet of heaven*

Double Fulfillment

Which expressions in the prophecy of Joel seem to imply a double fulfillment of this outpouring of the Spirit? "Be glad then, ye children of Zion, and rejoice in the LORD your God: for he hath given you the former rain moderately, and he will cause to come down for you the rain, the former rain, and the latter rain in the first *month*" (v. 23). In the East, the early rain falls to prepare the soil for seed sowing in the first season of the Jewish year, while the latter rain falls at the closing of the farming season to ripen the grain for harvest. The early rain was necessary for the seed to germinate.

In the process of seed germination, after a seed is planted, if the soil has no moisture or warmth, it remains dormant until after the rainy season has brought sufficient moisture. A seed has a coating that protects the primary embryo or seedling inside. The first sign of germination is the seed's absorption of water—lots of water—and as the hard cover begins to decay and the embryo gets larger, the coating bursts open and the growing plant emerges.

The tip of the root is the first thing to emerge. God designed the root to grow downward into the soil. The main job of the root is to help anchor the seed in place and allow the embryo to absorb water and nutrients from the surrounding soil. After this, the blade, ear, and full corn appear, and all this happens under the nourishing shower of the early rain.

From the agricultural model, a farmer needs rain at two crucial points in the growing cycle to produce a bountiful harvest, and this is called the early and latter rain. The early rain is needed before and right after the seed is planted. It helps cause the seed to germinate and produce a healthy crop. Then the crop needs the latter rain right before the harvest. It falls to ripen the grain and prepare it for harvest time, which shortly follows. After heavy showers of rain during the summer season there is a break. Excess rain during the growing season can cause crops to swell and split, develop mold and rot, or suffer quality loss.

At this break period, the sun appears, and the top of the soil dries out quickly. Then the soil gets warmth as the crops begin to ripen in preparation for the harvest. Afterward, it showers again for the last time and then ceases as we now slowly move into the time of harvest in the autumn season. "The Lord employs these operations of nature to represent the work of the Holy Spirit" (White 1923, p. 506).

Early Rain

"Then shall we know, *if* we follow on to know the LORD: his going forth is prepared as the morning; and he shall come unto us as the rain, as the latter *and* former rain unto the earth" (Hosea 6:3). Through these operations of nature God, is revealing the two-phase work of the Holy Spirit. The early outpouring of the Holy Spirit on the day of Pentecost prepared the world for the extensive sowing of the gospel seed.

In the parable of the sower, Christ illustrates the things of the kingdom of heaven. From the natural seed cast into the soil, Christ desires to lead our minds to the gospel seed. The Word of God is the seed. Every seed has in itself a germinating principle. In it, the life of the plant is encapsulated. Therefore, there is life in God's Word. Christ says, "It is the spirit that quickeneth; the flesh profiteth nothing: the words that I speak unto you, *they* are spirit, and *they* are life" (John 6:63).

The human heart is the soil. Without the Holy Spirit bringing divine moisture and warmth into our hearts, every seed will remain dormant. "As the dew and the rain are given first to cause the seed to germinate, and then to ripen the harvest, so the Holy Spirit is given to carry forward, from one stage to another, the process of spiritual growth" (White 1923, p. 506).

As the first sign of germination is the seed's absorption of water, so God designed that His Word in us would absorb the Holy Spirit. Just as lots of water helps the hard cover decay, the embryo gets larger, the coating bursts open, and the growing plant emerges, so the Holy Spirit is to destroy the old nature in preparation for the new nature in Christ to emerge in us.

Just as the tip of the root is the first thing to emerge, so God has designed the root to grow downward into the soil. The main job of the root is to help anchor the seed in place and allow the embryo to absorb water and nutrients from the surrounding soil. Similarly, we in our spiritual development and growth would take root downward before fruit bears upward. That's why the Scripture says, "And the remnant that is escaped of the house of Judah shall yet again take root downward, and bear fruit upward For out of Jerusalem shall go forth a remnant, and they that escape out of mount Zion: the zeal of the LORD *of hosts* shall do this" (2 Kings 19:30, 31).

"Many have in a great measure failed to receive the former rain. They have not obtained all the benefits that God has thus provided for them. They expect that the lack will be supplied by the latter rain. When the richest abundance of grace shall be bestowed, they intend to open their hearts to receive it. They are making a terrible mistake" (White 1923, p. 506).

The work that God has begun in the human heart in giving His light and knowledge must be continually going forward. Every individual must realize his or her necessity. The heart must be emptied of every defilement and cleansed for the indwelling of God's Spirit.

> When the Spirit of God takes possession of the heart, it transforms the life. Sinful thoughts are put away, evil deeds are renounced; love, humility, and peace take the place of anger, envy, and strife. Joy takes the place of sadness, and the countenance reflects the light of heaven. No one sees the hand that lifts the burden, or beholds the light descend from the courts above. The blessing comes when by faith the soul surrenders itself to God. Then that power which no human eye can see creates a new being in the image of God. (White, *The Desire of Ages*, p. 173)

Latter Rain

As was the early rain, so will be the latter rain. While we cherish the blessings of the early rain, we must not lose sight of the fact that without the latter rain to fill out the ears and ripen the grain, the harvest will not be ready for the sickle, and the labor of the sower will have been in vain. For what are we told to pray? "Ask ye of the LORD rain in the time of the latter rain; *so* the LORD shall make bright clouds, and give them showers of rain, to everyone grass in the field" (Zech. 10:1).

It was by confession and forsaking of sin and earnest prayer and consecration of themselves to God that the early disciples prepared for the outpouring of the Holy Spirit on the day of Pentecost. The same work, only to a greater degree, must be done now. Then we just have to ask for the blessing and wait for the Lord to perfect the work concerning us.

> It is God who began the work, and He will finish His work, making man complete in Jesus Christ. But there must be no neglect of the grace represented by the former rain. Only those who are living up to the light they have will receive greater light. Unless we are daily advancing in the exemplification of the active Christian virtues, we shall not recognize the manifestations of the Holy Spirit in the latter rain. It may be falling on hearts all around us, but we shall not discern or receive it. (White, *Testimonies to Ministers and Gosper Workers*, p. 507)

At no point in our experience can we dispense with the assistance of He who enables us to start the process. The blessings received under the former rain are needful to us until the end. However, these alone will not suffice. Why not? The baptism of the Holy Spirit under the latter rain will lead to a great revival of true religion and the performance of many remarkable works. Heavenly intelligences will come among us, and people will speak as they are moved by the Spirit of God.

"Thousands in the eleventh hour will see and acknowledge the truth.... These conversions to truth will be made with a rapidity that will surprise the church, and God's name alone will be glorified" (White 1958, p. 16).

"The Holy Spirit will come to all who are begging for the bread of life to give to their neighbors" (White 1901, p. 90).

"When we bring our hearts into unity with Christ, and our lives into harmony with His work, the Spirit that fell on the disciples on the day of Pentecost will fall on us" (White 1946, pp. 697, 698).

"Since this is the means by which we are to receive power, why do we not hunger and thirst for the gift of the Spirit? Why do we not talk of it, pray for it, and preach concerning it" (White 1911, p. 50)?

Dear friends, the time has finally arrived when we should ask for the second Pentecost individually and corporately. Those who are not filled with the Holy Spirit will be doomed. Time is running out. Why are we playing games with our souls?

Do you seek to glorify God and honor Him in your life? You should pursue and pray for a spirit of thankfulness for all the blessings you enjoy and plead earnestly for the Holy Spirit to dwell in you. If you do not possess the Holy Spirit, there is a fault, and it is in you, for Jesus says, "If ye, then, being evil, know how to give good gifts unto your children, how much more shall your heavenly Father give the Holy Spirit to them that ask him" (Luke 11:13).

With such an assurance of the willingness of your Father in heaven to give you the Holy Spirit, how can you remain away from him? How can you neglect to ask Him in confidence to perform that work in you so necessary to make you a devoted Christian? Oh, come to Jesus now, dear friends, with a broken heart and confidence in His mercy and promises. Plead for pardon for your past wanderings from His fold; earnestly pray until you feel His pardoning love and the fullness of His Spirit dwelling in you.

"The Holy Spirit, the representative of God, is the greatest of all gifts. All 'good things' are comprised in this. The Creator Himself can give us nothing greater, nothing better. When we beseech the Lord to pity us in our distress, and to guide us by His Holy Spirit, He will never turn away our prayer" (White 1988, p. 107).

It is possible even for a parent to turn away from his or her hungry child, but God can never reject the cry of the needy and longing heart. With such beautiful tenderness, He has described His love! To those who in days of darkness feel that God is unmindful of them, this is the message from the Father's heart: "Zion said, The Lord hath forsaken me, and my Lord hath forgotten me. Can a woman forget her sucking child, that she should not have compassion on the son of her womb? yea, they may forget, yet will I not forget thee. Behold, I have graven thee upon the palms of my hands" (Isa. 49:14–16).

> Every promise in the Word of God furnishes us with subject matter for prayer, presenting the pledged word of Jehovah as our assurance. Whatever spiritual blessing we need, it is our privilege to claim through Jesus. We may tell the Lord, with the simplicity of a child, exactly what we need. We may state to Him our temporal matters, asking Him for bread and raiment as well as for the bread of life and the robe of Christ's righteousness. Your heavenly Father knows that you have need of all these things, and you are invited to ask Him concerning them. It is through the name of Jesus that every favor is received. God will honor that name, and will supply your necessities from the riches of His liberality. (White, *Lift Him Up*, p. 107)

To be born of water and the Spirit describes two life experiences. Water baptism symbolically represents the cleansing of the physical life, while the baptism of the Holy Spirit is the resuscitation of the spiritual life. "For the daily baptism of the Spirit every worker should offer his petition to God. Companies of Christian workers should gather to ask for special help, for heavenly wisdom, that they may know how to plan and execute wisely. Especially should they pray that God will baptize His chosen ambassadors in mission fields with a rich measure of His Spirit" (White 1911, pp. 50, 51).

"The disciples did not ask for a blessing for themselves. They were weighted with the burden of souls. The gospel was to be carried to the ends of the earth, and they claimed the endowment of power that Christ had promised. Then it was that the Holy Spirit was poured out, and thousands were converted in a day" (White 1946, p. 699).

As Christ was glorified on the day of Pentecost, so will He again be glorified in the closing work of the gospel. John wrote, "And after these things I saw another angel come down from heaven, having great power; and the earth was lightened with his glory" (Rev. 18:1). The prophecies in Revelation 18 will soon be fulfilled.

The Spirit of the Lord will so graciously bless consecrated human instrumentalities that men, women, and children will open their lips in praise and thanksgiving, filling the earth with the knowledge of God and His unsurpassed glory, as the waters cover the much of the world.

"Those who have held the beginning of their confidence firm unto the end will be wide-awake during the time that the third angel's message is proclaimed with great power" (White 1976, p. 218).

I sincerely believe that there's no way for you to read these astonishing truths of God's Word without having a deep longing to follow Christ all the way and have a part in His glorious kingdom. I know that you would have never read this book unless you had a real interest in learning the truth and following Jesus all the way.

Does God want you, dear reader, to be His child? The answer is yes! Now the question is, do you want to be God's child? If your answer is yes, then by the authority of God's Word, you are a child of God. Put your hand into His and stay with Him. "Thou wilt keep him in perfect peace whose mind is stayed on thee: because he trusted in thee, trust ye in the Lord forever: for in the Lord Jehovah is everlasting strength" (Isa. 26:3, 4)

BIBLIOGRAPHY

"Defining Spiritualism." Natural Spiritualist Association of Churches, http://1ref.us/r1, (accessed 11/15/2018).

"Mantra Meditation." Yogapedia, http://1ref.us/qy, (accessed 11/15/2018).

"Missions and Expansion." Patheos, http://1ref.us/qu, (accessed 11/15/2018).

"Modern Age." Patheos, http://1ref.us/qv, (accessed 11/15/2018).

"What Is Mantra Meditation." Mindworks, http://1ref.us/qz, (accessed 11/15/2018).

"What Is Zen?" Zen Buddhism, http://1ref.us/r0, (accessed 11/15/2018).

Ankerberg, John, and John Weldon. *Fast Facts on Roman Catholicism*. Eugene, OR: Harvest House Publishers, 2004.

Ann Pietrangelo. "Left Brain vs. Right Brain: What Does This Mean for Me?" Healthline, http://1ref.us/qr, (accessed 11/15/2018).

Concise Oxford English Dictionary.

Desmond, Shaw. *Psychic Pitfalls*. London: Rider and Company, 1954.

Edwards, Tilden. *Spiritual Friend: Reclaiming the Gift of Spiritual Direction*. Paulist Press, 1980.

Froom, LeRoy Edwin. *The Conditionalist Faith of Our Fathers*. Hagerstown, MD: Review and Herald Publishing Association, 1965.

Fowkes, Steven. Quora. http://1ref.us/qs (accessed 11/15/2018).

Jefferson. "The facts about masturbation (Try to prove me wrong)." SexualReboot, http://1ref.us/r2, (accessed 1/15/2018).

Makransky, John. "Buddhist Reflections on Theological Learning and Spiritual Discipline." Religious Studies News, http://1ref.us/r3, (accessed 11/15/2018).

Maples, Rebeka. "Spiritual Formation." Course of Study School of Ohio, http://1ref.us/qw, (accessed 11/15/2018).

Martin, Malachi. *The Jesuits*. Bloomington, IN: Simon & Schuster, 1988.

McKie, Robin. "Fasting Can Help Protect Against Brain Diseases, Scientists Say," *The Guardian*. http://1ref.us/rn (accessed 2/27/2019).

Missett, Bill. *Awakening the Soul*, Book 2. Bloomington, IN: AuthorHouse, 2005.

Mulinde, John. "How Satan Stops Our Prayers," *Divine Revelations*. http://1ref.us/rm (accessed 2/27/2019).

Paul II, John. *Crossing the Threshold of Hope*. New York: Knopf, 1995.

Panjwani, Mush. "11 Health Benefits of Fasting." http://1ref.us/ro (accessed 2/27/2019).

Synan, Vinson. *The Holiness-Pentecostal Movement in the United States*. Grand Rapids, MI: Eerdmans, 1971.

The American Heritage Dictionary.

Uzorma, Prof. Iyke Nathan. *Occult Grand Master Now in Christ*, vol. 1. Bloomington, IN: Xlibris, 2013.

Wagner, C. Peter. *Your Spiritual Gifts Can Help Your Church Grow*. Glendale, CA: Regal Books, 1979.

Watch Tower Bible and Tract Society of Pennsylvania. *Mankind's Search for God*. Wallkill, NY: Watch Tower Bible and Tract Society, 1990.

White, Ellen G. "A Teacher Sent from God," *The Review and Herald*, April 30, 1901.

White, Ellen G. "Have You Oil in Your Vessels With Your Lamps?" *The Review and Herald*, September 17, 1895.

White, Ellen G. "Obedience the Fruit of Union with Christ," *The Review and Herald*, September 3, 1901.

White, Ellen G. "Our Guide-book," *The Signs of the Times*, June 26, 1901.

White, Ellen G. "Our Sacrifice," *The Signs of the Times*, December 8, 1898.

White, Ellen G. "The Blessing of Obedience," *The Signs of the Times*, January 25, 1899.

White, Ellen G. "The Bread of Life," *The Signs of the Times*, October 3, 1900.

White, Ellen G. "The Faith That Will Stand the Test," *The Review and Herald*, January 10, 1888.

White, Ellen G. "The Necessity of Receiving the Holy Spirit," *The Signs of the Times*, August 1, 1892.

White, Ellen G. *Christian Experience and Teachings of Ellen G. White*. Mountain View, CA: Pacific Press Publishing Association, 1922.

White, Ellen G. *Conflict and Courage*. Washington, DC: Review and Herald Publishing Association, 1970.

White, Ellen G. *Counsels on Diet and Foods*. Washington, DC: Review and Herald Publishing Association, 1938.

White, Ellen G. *Darkness Before Dawn*. Nampa, ID: Pacific Press Publishing Association, 1997.

White, Ellen G. *Early Writings*. Washington, DC: Review and Herald Publishing Association, 1882.

White, Ellen G. *Evangelism*. Washington, DC: Review and Herald Publishing Association, 1946.

White, Ellen G. *God's Amazing Grace*. Washington, DC: Review and Herald Publishing Association, 1973.

White, Ellen G. *Gospel Workers*. Washington, DC: Review and Herald Publishing Association, 1915.

White, Ellen G. *Healthful Living*. Battle Creek, MI: Medical Missionary Board, 1897.

White, Ellen G. *In Heavenly Places*. Washington, DC: Review and Herald Publishing Association, 1967.

White, Ellen G. *Lift Him Up*. Hagerstown, MD: Review and Herald Publishing Association, 1988.

White, Ellen G. *Manuscript Releases*. Vol. 4. Silver Spring, MD: Ellen G. White Estate, 1990.

White, Ellen G. *Manuscript Releases*. Vol. 5. Silver Spring, MD: Ellen G. White Estate, 1990.

White, Ellen G. *Manuscript Releases*. Vol. 9. Silver Spring, MD: Ellen G. White Estate, 1990.

White, Ellen G. *Maranatha*. Washington, DC: Review and Herald Publishing Association, 1976.

White, Ellen G. *Messages to Young People*. Hagerstown, MD: Review and Herald Publishing Association, 1930.

White, Ellen G. *Mind, Character, and Personality.* Vol. 2. Nashville, TN: Southern Publishing Association, 1977.

White, Ellen G. *My Life Today.* Washington, DC: Review and Herald Publishing Association, 1952.

White, Ellen G. Our Father Cares. Hagerstown, MD: Review and Herald Publishing Association, 1991.

White, Ellen G. *Patriarchs and Prophets.* Washington, DC: Review and Herald Publishing Association, 1890.

White, Ellen G. *Prayer.* Nampa, ID: Pacific Press Publishing Association, 2002.

White, Ellen G. *Selected Messages.* Book 1. Washington, DC: Review and Herald Publishing Association, 1958.

White, Ellen G. *Selected Messages.* Book 2. Washington, DC: Review and Herald Publishing Association, 1958.

White, Ellen G. *Selected Messages.* Book 3. Washington, DC: Review and Herald Publishing Association, 1980.

White, Ellen G. *Sons and Daughters of God.* Washington, DC: Review and Herald Publishing Association, 1955.

White, Ellen G. *The Southern Watchman*, January 1, 1903.

White, Ellen G. *Spiritual Gifts.* Vol. 4b. Battle Creek, MI: Seventh-day Adventist Publishing Association, 1864.

White, Ellen G. *Steps to Christ*. Mountain View, CA: Pacific Press Publishing Association, 1892.

White, Ellen G. *Temperance.* Mountain View, CA: Pacific Press Publishing Association, 1949.

White, Ellen G. *Testimonies for the Church*. Vol. 1. Mountain View, CA: Pacific Press Publishing Association, 1868.

White, Ellen G. *Testimonies for the Church*. Vol. 5. Mountain View, CA: Pacific Press Publishing Association, 1889.

White, Ellen G. *Testimonies for the Church*. Vol. 6. Mountain View, CA: Pacific Press Publishing Association, 1901.

White, Ellen G. *Testimonies to Ministers and Gospel Workers*. Mountain View, CA: Pacific Press Publishing Association, 1923.

White, Ellen G. *Testimony Studies on Diet and Foods.* Loma Linda, CA: College of Medical Evangelists, 1926.

White, Ellen G. *The Acts of the Apostles*. Mountain View, CA: Pacific Press Publishing Association, 1911.

White, Ellen G. *The Adventist Home*. Hagerstown, MD: Review and Herald Publishing Association, 1952.

White, Ellen G. *The Desire of Ages*. Mountain View, CA: Pacific Press Publishing Association, 1898.

White, Ellen G. *The Faith I Live By*. Washington, DC: Review and Herald Publishing Association, 1958.

White, Ellen G. *The Great Controversy*. Mountain View, CA: Pacific Press Publishing Association, 1911.

White, Ellen G. *The Ministry of Healing*. Mountain View, CA: Pacific Press Publishing Association, 1905.

White, Ellen G. *The Sanctified Life*. Washington, DC: Review and Herald Publishing Association, 1937.

White, Ellen G. *The SDA Bible Commentary*. Vol. 4. Washington, DC: Review and Herald Publishing Association, 1955.

White, Ellen G. *The SDA Bible Commentary*. Vol. 6. Washington, DC: Review and Herald Publishing Association, 1956.

White, Ellen G. *The SDA Bible Commentary*. Vol. 7. Washington, DC: Review and Herald Publishing Association, 1957.

White, Ellen G. *The Spirit of Prophecy*. Vol. 4. Battle Creek, MI: Seventh-day Adventist Publishing Association, 1884.

We invite you to view the complete
selection of titles we publish at:
www.TEACHServices.com

We encourage you to write us
with your thoughts about this,
or any other book we publish at:
info@TEACHServices.com

TEACH Services' titles may be purchased in
bulk quantities for educational, fund-raising,
business, or promotional use.
bulksales@TEACHServices.com

Finally, if you are interested in seeing
your own book in print, please contact us at:
publishing@TEACHServices.com

We are happy to review your manuscript at no charge.

www.ingramcontent.com/pod-product-compliance
Lightning Source LLC
Chambersburg PA
CBHW070554160426
43199CB00014B/2504

9 781479 609994